50 Spectacular Salads

STEP-BY-STEP

50 Spectacular Salads

Steven Wheeler

Photography by Edward Allwright

SMITHMARK

© Anness Publishing Limited 1994

All rights reserved. No part of this publication may be
reproduced, stored in a retrieval system, or transmitted in
any way or by any means, electronic, mechanical,
photocopying, recording or otherwise, without the prior
permission of the copyright holder.

This edition published in 1994 by
SMITHMARK Publishers Inc.
16 East 32nd Street
New York
NY 10016

SMITHMARK books are available for bulk purchase for sales
promotion and for premium use. For details write or call
the manager of special sales, SMITHMARK Publishers Inc.
16 East 32nd Street, New York, 10016; (212) 532–6600

ISBN 0 8317 6516 X

Produced by Anness Publishing Limited
1 Boundary Row
London SE1 8HP

Printed and bound in Italy by Graphicom S.r.l., Vicenza

CONTENTS

INTRODUCTION

A well made salad is almost lyrical in its combination of fresh tastes, textures and colors expressing a particular mood or theme. This book looks at a variety of salad themes and shows that there is more to salads than meets the eye.

Seasonal changes are important and provide a useful lead when you are searching for inspiration. The finest salads begin with one or two ingredients that may catch the attention. If you come across a butter-rich pear, partner it with a handful of toasted pecan nuts, a few leaves of young spinach, and combine with a blue cheese dressing. If a freshly boiled crab takes your fancy, consider the rich flavors of avocado, cilantro leaves, and lime. Some new potatoes and young lettuce leaves will make it a salad to remember.

Most salads fit into the summer season and are inspired by an abundance of freshness and color. Summer salads are best eaten outdoors. In fall and winter we move inside to enjoy the warm flavors of wild mushrooms, duck breast, and chicken livers. The richness of these ingredients combines especially well with hearty leaves of oak leaf lettuce, escarole, and Belgian endive. Spring sees the arrival of young vegetables and tender salad leaves: lamb's lettuce, spinach, and arugula. These delicate flavors marry best with simply grilled fish, eggs, ham, and chicken. At the back of this book is a special index linked to ingredients you are most likely to have in store. From it you can decide which salad is most practical to make.

Simplicity is the key to a successful salad. Where two or more ingredients combine, their flavors should marry well together but should also still be individually identifiable. May your salads bring good health and happiness to your table!

Salad Vegetables

The salad vegetable is any type that earns its keep in a salad by virtue of freshness and flavor. Vegetables for a salad can be raw or lightly cooked. If cooked, they are best served warm or at room temperature to bring out their full flavor. No amount of guesswork can replace a sound knowledge of which vegetables partner most effectively.

Celery is a useful salad vegetable and is grown year round for its robust earthy flavor. The crisp stems should be neither stringy nor tough. Celery partners well with cooked ham, apple, and walnut in Waldorf Salad. It also belongs with Swiss cheese, chicken, and tongue.

Bulb, or Florence, fennel has a strong aniseed flavor and looks like a squat head of celery. From its center it puts forth soft green fronds that can be chopped and used as a herb. Because the flavor of the vegetable can be dominant, it may be blanched in boiling water for 6 minutes before use in a salad.

The turnip is grown for its tender tops and clean white root. When young, the bulbous root has a peppery sweetness. Its flavor marries well with creamed horseradish and caraway seed and is an excellent partner to cold roast beef.

The cucumber is a common salad ingredient and turns up, invited or not, in salad bowls everywhere. The robust quality of this vegetable is best appreciated in strongly flavored salads.

Fresh garlic is essential to the cooking of South America, Asia, and the Mediterranean. Strong in taste, garlic promotes good health and a vigorous appetite. To moderate the strength of fresh garlic, store crushed cloves in olive oil and use the oil sparingly in salad dressings.

The scallion has a milder flavor than the common onion and gives a gentle bite to many popular salads. The mature variety has a stronger flavor than younger onions.

Mushrooms provide a rich tone to many salads and are eaten both raw and cooked. The oyster mushroom, which grows wild in late summer and autumn, has a fine flavor and texture. This and other wild varieties are often cultivated in a semi-wild environment to meet consumer demand. White and brown button mushrooms combine well with fresh garlic, herbs, and butter.

Tomatoes play an important part in salads and are valued for flavor and color. Dwarf varieties usually ripen more quickly than large ones and tend to have a better flavor.

There are three main varieties of onion that are suited to salads. The strongest, pictured here, is the small brown onion. It should be chopped finely and used sparingly. Less strong are the Spanish and vidalia onions, which may be coarsely chopped.

The avocado has a smooth buttery flesh when ripe and is an asset to many salads, of which Guacamole is perhaps the best known. Avocados are rich in calories and are a good source of potassium and B group vitamins.

Before sweet corn is fully grown, the baby cobs can be lightly cooked or eaten raw and should be served warm or at room temperature with other young vegetables.

Zucchini can sometimes be bitter. It is usually cooked before being combined with other young vegetables. Smooth in texture when cooked, zucchini marry wonderfully with tomatoes, eggplant, bell peppers, and onions.

Carrots should be young, slender and sweet to taste. Either cooked or raw, they bring flavor and color to a salad. Raw carrots are a valuable source of vitamin A and are rich in minerals.

The varieties of green bean are too numerous to mention here, but they all have their merits as salad vegetables. To appreciate the sweet flavor of green beans, cook them for no longer than 6 minutes. Properly cooked green beans should squeak between the teeth when bitten into.

Left: *Almost any vegetable can be used in a salad, either raw or lightly cooked. You will only need a limited number of ingredients to create a successful salad if you choose complementary flavors.*

Selecting Fruit

The contents of the fruit bowl offers endless possibilities for sweet and savory salads. Sweet fruit salads are probably the best known, although in these, individual fruits are inclined to get lost in a multi-colored muddle where varieties merge into one flavor. When preparing a fruit salad, aim to combine both flavors and colors in such a way that the dish looks and tastes as appetizing as possible. When choosing fruit, make sure that it tastes as good as it looks. If fruit is fresh and ripe, it has every reason to taste good.

A knowledge of which fruits combine most effectively is essential if you are going to make your own salad combinations. The flavor of ripe pineapple, for example, combines best with strawberries, lychees, and oranges; other tropical fruits belong with pineapple, but few bring out its sweetness as well. Pineapples are available year round, but are best in May and June. Ripe pineapples resist firm pressure when squeezed and have a sweet smell.

Bananas bring a special richness to fruit salads, although their distinct flavor can often interfere with more delicate fruit. Lightly grilled, bananas are delicious with a salad of barbecued chicken, bacon, sweet corn, and tart leaves of watercress. Under-ripe yellow bananas are not easily digested: make sure that the skin is mottled brown but free from bruising.

A bunch of grapes on the table is almost a dessert in itself. Large Muscat varieties, whose season runs from late summer to autumn, are the most coveted and also the most expensive. When thoroughly chilled and served alongside a frozen granita of Muscat wine, Muscat grapes make an impressive dessert.

When in season, oranges have a bright challenging flavor. Citrus fruits are at their best during winter when individual fruits feel heavy for their size. Oranges are best segmented and added to sweet and savory salads. Their sharpness balances the richness of many fish salads.

Unusual tropical fruits import character to exotic salads. The visually dramatic pithaya offers little flavor, but is appreciated for its luscious black and white interior. Some varieties of this South American cactus fruit have a crimson-pink flesh.

The mango and the pawpaw or papaya are two fruits that lend themselves to exotic salads. Mangoes show a red blush when ripe. Pawpaws become yellow-green and yield to firm pressure when squeezed gently.

Apples and pears grow in temperate climates as far south as Argentina and Cape Town. Both fruits offer a unique flavor to sweet and savory salads. Ripe pears taste especially good with strong blue cheese and toasted pecan nuts in a savory salad. Apples find favor in a Waldorf Salad with ham, celery, and walnuts.

Melons grow in abundance from mid to late summer and provide a source of freshness and flavor. Pictured here is watermelon, the largest variety with the most succulent flavor; and galia and charentais, which have a sweeter, more penetrating fragrance. Melon is at its most delicious served icy cold.

The raspberry is a much-coveted soft fruit that partners well with ripe mango, passion fruit, and strawberries.

The strawberry, one of the most popular summer fruits, is best eaten at room temperature with sugar and cream.

Wild blackberries are at their best from late summer to autumn when they can be found in the countryside. Cultivated varieties are available but have a less dramatic flavor. The blackberry, a member of the rose family, is delicious served with a granita of rose water.

Blueberries are everyone's favorite fruit stirred into pancakes, but these firm-fleshed berries are also delicious in an unusual salad with orange and lavender meringue. Blueberries enjoy the sharpness of fresh oranges. Cultivated blueberries are sold from spring to autumn, but wild varieties are the most flavorsome.

Right: *Fresh fruits can be used in both sweet and savory salads. Ensure they are ripe and in peak condition.*

Salad Leaves

Arugula
Argula has a pepper-rich taste of lemon and is often combined with milder leaves to add flavor and zest. Arugula leaves keep well when immersed in cold water.

Batavia
The Batavia has a bitter flavor similar to escarole but a slightly sweeter, softer taste. It is suited to most salads and stands up to a well-flavored dressing.

Escarole
Escarole is a robust green salad leaf that, like curly endive and Belgian endive, has a bitter flavor. It is best during the winter months and is usually served with a sweet dressing.

Frisée lettuce
Frisée is a member of the chicory family. It has a clean bitter taste that combines well with sweeter salad leaves.

Iceberg lettuce
The tightly packed iceberg lettuce has a crisp texture, with little flavor of its own. It is suited to fine shredding and combines well with strong dressings and other salad leaves.

Lamb's lettuce
Lamb's lettuce, or mâche, grows year round in small fragile shoots. These are eaten whole and have a mild sweet flavor.

Little gem
Little gem is a small, sweet compact lettuce similar in flavor to romaine. Its well-formed leaves are inclined to keep longer than those of many other lettuce varieties, a useful trait.

Lollo biondo
Lollo biondo or green lollo is a loose-leaf lettuce with a curly edge. It has a mild flavor and belongs with stronger-tasting lettuce leaves.

Lollo rosso
Lollo rosso or red lollo is a mild-flavored lettuce with a curly edge. This loose-leaf variety is appreciated for its purple-red tint.

Oak-leaf lettuce
The broad wavy leaves of oak-leaf, or feuille de chêne, are tinted a purple-brown. Its dark color and mild taste go well with the bitter leaves of escarole and frisée.

Romaine
Romaine lettuce, which originated on the Greek island of Cos, has a robust slightly bitter flavor. Romaine is the preferred salad leaf for Caesar salad.

Spinach
Young spinach leaves, used in many salads, are appreciated for their rich sweet flavor. If the leaves are large, the stems should be removed before washing.

Watercress
Watercress, which has a tart peppery taste, is a member of the mustard family. Its strong flavor combines especially well with eggs, fish, and grilled meats.

lollo rosso

Batavia

frisée lettuce

lollo biondo

escarole

little gem

romaine

iceberg lettuce

arugula

spinach

oak-leaf lettuce

watercress

lamb's lettuce

Dressing Ingredients

The best-dressed salads are those that allow individual ingredients to taste of themselves. Too many salads are ruined with badly made dressings in which vinegar dominates. An excess of vinegar drowns the quality of a salad and also plays havoc with any wine that is served with it.

Oil is the main ingredient of most dressings and provides an important richness to salads. Most of the salad oil used today is taken from the seed or kernel of the sunflower, safflower, peanut, or soy bean. These neutral oils have little flavor and are ideally used as a background for stronger oils. Sesame, walnut, and hazelnut oils are the strongest and should be used sparingly. Olive oil is prized for its clarity of flavor and clean richness. The most significant producers of olive oil are Italy, France, Spain, and Greece. These and other countries produce three main grades of olive oil: estate-grown extra-virgin olive oil, for which olives have been hand-picked and cold-pressed to give an individual flavor; virgin olive oil, for which olives have been mechanically picked and often warmed before pressing to extract a higher percentage of oil; and semi-fine olive oil, of an ordinary standard best suited to high-temperature frying. Many extra-virgin olive oils compare with château-bottled wines. They tend to be expensive and reflect individual character and taste. It is best to reflect the nationality of a salad by using an oil of the same country.

Garlic oil

Garlic oil is made by steeping 4–5 crushed cloves of garlic in a neutral-flavored oil. The oil can then be used to impart a gentle garlic taste to salad dressings of many kinds. Garlic oil is also useful when frying bread croutons.

Olive oils

French olive oils are subtly flavored and provide a well-balanced lightness to dressings. The golden oil featured here has a sweet fruity flavor and is suited to the foods of southern France.

Greek olive oils are typically strong in character. They are often green with a thick texture and are unsuitable for mayonnaise.

Italian olive oils are noted for their vigorous Mediterranean flavors and suggest grassy herbs – often a prickly taste of black pepper. Tuscan oils are noted for their well-rounded spicy flavor and are often green in color. Sicilian oils tend to be lighter in texture, although they are often more strongly flavored than Tuscan oils.

Spanish olive oils are typically fruity and often have a nutty quality with a pleasant bitterness.

Nut oils

Hazelnut and walnut oils are valued for their strong nutty flavor. Tasting richly of the nuts from which they are pressed, both are usually blended with neutral oils for salad dressings.

Seed oils

Peanut oil and sunflower oil are valued by many cooks for their clean neutral flavor. These and other seed oils – safflower, soy, and grapeseed – are used in conjunction with stronger oils. However, corn oil is considered to be too sweet and cloying for salad use.

Vinegars

White-wine vinegar is probably the most popular type for salad dressings, but it should be used in moderation to balance the richness of an oil. There are many other vinegars from which to choose; however, a good-quality white-wine vinegar will serve most purposes.

Capers

Capers are the pickled flower buds of a bush native to the Mediterranean. Their strong sharp flavor is well suited to richly flavored salads. Smaller, tightly packed capers are more intensely flavored than larger varieties.

Lemon and lime juice

The juice of lemons and limes is used to impart a clean acidity to oil dressings. Both have a similar strength to vinegar and should be used in moderation.

Mustard

Mustard has a tendency to bring out the flavor of other ingredients. It acts as an emulsifier in dressings and allows oil and vinegar to merge for a short period of time. Where possible French, German, and English mustards should be used for salads of the same nationality.

Olives

Black and green olives belong in salads that take their flavor from the sun. Black olives are generally sweeter than green ones, although many green olives are treated with sugar and sometimes lemon juice to encourage their flavor.

Italian olive oil

Spanish olive

lemons

Italian olive oil

French olive oil

Italian olive oil

safflower oil

hazelnut oil

walnut oil

peanut oil

garlic oil

white-wine vinegar

limes

olives

capers

mustard

Using Herbs

For as long as salads draw on the qualities of fresh produce, sweet herbs have an important part to play in providing individual character and flavor. The word fresh is used here to imply that salad ingredients are alive with flavor. When herbs are used in a salad, they should be as full of life as the salad leaves they accompany. Dried herbs are no substitute for fresh ones and should be kept for stews and casseroles. Salad herbs are distinguished by their ability to release flavor without lengthy cooking. Most salad herbs belong

finely chopped in salad dressings and marinades, while the robust flavors of rosemary, thyme and fennel branches can be used on the barbecue to impart a smoky herb flavor to meat and fish. Ideally salad herbs should be picked just before use, but if you cannot use them immediately, keep them in water to retain their freshness. Parsley, mint, and cilantro will keep for up to 1 week in this way if also covered with a plastic bag and placed in the refrigerator.

Garden mint is the most common mint variety. Others

include spearmint, with its jagged leaf edge, and apple mint, which has a round leaf shape. The flavor of mint is unusual because it distinguishes and cleanses other flavors instead of merging with them. Mint is widely used in Greek and Middle Eastern salads, such as Tzatziki and Tabbouleh, to provide a clean refreshing flavor.

Basil, a summer herb related to mint, is remarkable for its fresh pungent flavor. Its aniseed-clove fragrance is released by rubbing a few leaves in the hand. It is the signature of many Italian dishes, but appears throughout the Mediterranean in a variety of salad dishes. Dried basil is no substitute for the fresh herb.

Fresh thyme is an asset to salads that feature rich, earthy flavors. Native to southern Europe, it has a penetrating minty lemon flavor. The two main varieties are broad-leaf English and narrow-leaf French thyme. Both are used in conjunction with parsley, garlic, marjoram, and lavender to create Mediterranean flavors.

Flat- and curly-leaf parsley are both grown for their fresh green flavor — reminiscent of carrot, celery, and caraway. Flat-leaf parsley is said to have a stronger taste and is certainly easier to

chop. More than just a garnish, freshly chopped parsley is used by the handful in salads and salad dressings, especially those that contain garlic. Dried parsley is not suitable for salads.

Chives are a member of the onion family and have a mild onion flavor. The slender green stems, which grow wild in wet meadows, belong with the scent of summer garlic. Chives produce a soft magenta flower that is edible. Freeze-dried chives are available, but are not recommended for salad use.

Fresh lavender is native to the rocky hills of the Mediterranean and has been enjoyed since Greek and Roman times for its soothing fragrance. All lavender is edible and combines naturally with thyme, garlic, marjoram, honey, and orange. As a marinade, this combination is delicious with a grilled chicken salad. Lavender's association with orange enables us to enjoy it in a fruit salad of blueberry and meringue.

Although it is not technically a herb, the sweet-scented rose can be used to flavor fresh fruit salads. The blackberry and raspberry are members of the rose family, an association that allows their characters to mingle.

Left: *Flavorful additions to salads include (clockwise from top left) thyme, flat-leaf parsley, chives, lavender, rose petals, mint, and basil.*

Using Spices

Spices are the aromatic seasonings found in the seed, bark, fruit, and sometimes flowers of certain plants and trees. The value of spices has been appreciated in Europe since the Arabs first monopolized the Eastern spice trade over 3,000 years ago. Prices remained high until ocean trade was established by Britain in the seventeenth century. Today we still value spices for their warm inviting flavors, and thankfully their price is relatively low. The flavor of spice is contained in the volatile oils of the seed, bark, or fruit; so like herbs, spices should be used as fresh as possible. Whole spices keep better than ground ones, which tend to lose their freshness in 3–4 months.

Not all spices are suitable for salad making, although many allow us to explore the flavors of other cultures. The recipes in this book use curry spices – coriander, cumin, cardamom, cinnamon, chili, and turmeric – in moderation so as not to spoil the delicate salad flavors. The moderate use of Indian spices is often found in French cooking when spices are employed with respect for underlying flavor.

Pepper, the most popular spice used in the West, features in the cooking of almost every nation. Freshly ground pepper serves to excite the taste buds, thus increasing our awareness of taste sensation. Pepper is the fruit of a tropical vine, native to the forests of monsoon Asia, but today it is grown as far west as Madagascar. The berries are picked in clusters when green, and drying develops their black color. Black peppercorns have the mildest flavor and should always be freshly ground in a mill. Both salt and pepper should be added to a salad after it is dressed.

Cayenne pepper is the dried and finely ground fruit of a hot chili. It has a similar effect on the taste buds as the peppercorn and is an important seasoning in South American cooking. Cayenne pepper is used in preference to black or white pepper when seasoning fish and shellfish. If the ground cayenne is too hot, it can be blended with mild paprika. Care should be taken when using cayenne pepper – its taste is powerful and a little goes a long way.

Celery salt is a combination of celery seed and salt. It is usually sold ready-made, although you can make your own by pounding equal volumes of celery seed and fine salt in a pestle and mortar. If celery seed is not available, lovage seed, which has a strong celery taste, can be substituted. Celery salt is most often used when seasoning vegetables, in particular carrots with which celery has a strong association. Care should be taken not to over-salt when trying to impart a celery flavor.

Right: *A little spice goes a long way in salad making. Spices include (clockwise from top left) celery salt, caraway seeds, curry paste, saffron, black peppercorns, cayenne pepper.*

Caraway seeds are widely used in German, Alsatian, and Austrian cooking and feature strongly in many Jewish dishes. The small ribbed seeds are similar in appearance and taste to cumin and have a savory-sweet quality, thought to aid digestion. The flavor of caraway combines especially well with German mustard in a dressing for Frankfurter Salad.

Prepared curry paste is the best medium in which to preserve the flavor of Indian spices; it keeps better than blended powder, which is inclined to go stale. Madras paste has a good medium strength. Curry spices combine especially well in dressings and show off the sweet qualities of fish and shellfish.

Saffron, the world's most expensive spice, is made from the dried red-orange stigma of a purple-flowering crocus traditionally grown in Spain. Real saffron has a tobacco-rich smell and gives a sweet yellow tint to liquids used for cooking. There are many imitations which provide color without the flavor of the real thing. Saffron can be used in rich creamy dressings and brings out the richness of fresh seafood.

Equipment

Cheese grater
A sturdy cheese grater is widely used by the salad maker for grating hard-cooked eggs, vegetables, and the outer zest of citrus fruit.

Food processor
The food processor is useful for mixing and blending salad ingredients. Most have an attachment for slicing and grating large quantities.

Knives
Chopping and paring knives are subject to personal choice and should feel comfortable in the hand. Large chopping knives should be handled with care and respect for their sharpness.

Measuring cups and spoons
Measuring cups and spoons are useful for accurately gauging the volume and corresponding weight of salad ingredients. Spoon measures range from ½ tsp to 1 tbsp and cups from ¼ cup to 1 cup.

Mixing bowls
An assortment of glass mixing bowls that fit neatly inside each other are useful for a number of salad preparations.

Salad bowl
A sensibly shaped salad bowl with sloping sides is most practical for tossing salad leaves. Two large spoons are best for serving.

Saucepan
A good stainless-steel saucepan is a sound investment for any cook. The best pans are sold individually rather than as a set. They are expensive but will last a lifetime of simmering, blanching, and boiling.

Screw-top jar
A screw-top jar is most practical for making and storing salad dressings. Make sure that the jar has a tight-fitting lid.

Whisk
A sturdy whisk is useful for combining dressing ingredients smoothly. The best whisks are made of stainless steel and have a secure, hard plastic handle.

salad bowl

saucepan

mixing bowls

cheese grater

food processor

whisk

knives

measuring cups and spoons

screw-top jar

The Kitchen Herb Garden

During spring and summer many cooks like to grow their own supply of fresh herbs and salad leaves. A small garden planted in a sunny spot near the kitchen allows you to gather fresh produce as and when you need it. The extent of a kitchen garden can range from a few pots to an open soil bed. Most cooks enjoy the freshness and convenience of a few herbs growing in pots by the window, and may be tempted to raise unusual varieties from seed.

Planting seeds

Every packet of seeds carries instructions for planting. If you are growing herbs and salad leaves for the window sill, you can germinate seeds in partitioned trays and transfer the plants, as they grow, to well-drained pots until they are large enough to be planted in the garden. Regular watering and plenty of sun will ensure an abundance of freshness and flavor. Tomatoes can be grown from seed, but most gardeners prefer to buy young plants. Tomato plants do well even on a patio or terrace and are best positioned against a south-facing wall. Vegetables such as carrots, radishes, beet, and turnips are best planted in an open bed of rich soil. Seedlings that grow too close together should be thinned to enable proper development. Young thinnings are delicious in fresh colorful salads.

Growing in pots

If you have only a small garden, salad leaves and herbs can be grown successfully in terracotta pots. Regular watering is important and all pots should allow for drainage. For a constant supply of lettuce, sow seeds at 2-week intervals throughout the summer and pick when needed. In colder weather, herbs and salad leaves should be kept under glass to maximize warmth from the sun. Many herbs enjoy a sunny spot on an inside window ledge.

Picking and storing herbs

When herbs are picked, every effort should be made to keep their flavor intact. In season, bunches of parsley, mint, cilantro, and chives keep well in water. Covered with a plastic bag, these herbs will keep in the refrigerator for up to 1 week. Herbs such as thyme, rosemary, and lavender are suitable for slow drying in a well-ventilated cupboard. Dried herbs will keep for several months.

Above right: *Seeds can be grown in small trays on the window sill, and then transplanted to individual pots. When they are large enough, plant them in the garden.*

Right: *Herbs include (clockwise from top right) flat-leaf parsley, lavender, thyme, and chives.*

Opposite: *If space is at a premium, salad leaves and herbs can be grown successfully on the window sill.*

Mayonnaise

Mayonnaise is a simple emulsion made with egg yolks and oil. For consistent results, ensure that both egg yolks and oil are at room temperature before combining – around 70°F. Homemade mayonnaise is made with raw egg yolks and may therefore be considered unsuitable for young children, pregnant mothers, and the elderly.

Makes about 1 1/2 cups

INGREDIENTS
2 egg yolks
1 tsp French mustard
2/3 cup extra-virgin olive oil, French or
   Italian
2/3 cup peanut or sunflower oil
2 tsp white-wine vinegar
salt and pepper

1 Place the egg yolks and mustard in a food processor and blend smoothly.

2 Add the olive oil a little at a time while the processor is running. When the mixture is thick, add the remainder of the oil in a slow steady stream.

3 Add the vinegar and season to taste with salt and pepper.

COOK'S TIP

Should mayonnaise separate during blending, add 2 tbsp boiling water and beat until smooth. Store mayonnaise in the refrigerator for up to 1 week, sealed in a screw-top jar.

Blue Cheese and Chive Dressing

Blue cheese dressings have a strong robust flavor and are well suited to winter salad leaves: escarole, Belgian endive, and radicchio.

Makes about 1 3/4 cups

INGREDIENTS
3 oz blue cheese, Stilton, Bleu
   d'Auvergne, or Gorgonzola
2/3 cup low-fat plain yogurt
3 tbsp olive oil, preferably Italian
2 tbsp lemon juice
1 tbsp chopped fresh chives
black pepper

2 Add the remainder of the yogurt, the olive oil, and lemon juice.

1 Remove the rind from the cheese. Place the cheese with a third of the yogurt in a mixing bowl and combine smoothly with a wooden spoon.

3 Stir in the chives and season to taste with freshly ground black pepper.

French Dressing

French vinaigrette is the most widely used salad dressing and is appreciated for its simplicity and style. For the best flavor, use the finest extra-virgin olive oil and go easy on the vinegar.

Makes about ¹/₂ cup

INGREDIENTS
¹/₃ cup extra-virgin olive oil, French or
    Italian
1 tbsp white-wine vinegar
1 tsp French mustard
pinch of superfine sugar

2 Add the mustard and sugar.

1 Place the olive oil and vinegar in a screw-top jar.

3 Replace the lid and shake well.

French Herb Dressing

The delicate scents of fresh herbs combine especially well in a French dressing. Toss with a simple green salad and serve with good cheese and wine.

Makes about ¹/₂ cup

INGREDIENTS
4 tbsp extra-virgin olive oil, French or
    Italian
2 tbsp peanut or sunflower oil
1 tbsp lemon juice
4 tbsp finely chopped fresh herbs:
    parsley, chives, tarragon, and
    marjoram
pinch of superfine sugar

2 Add the lemon juice, herbs, and sugar.

1 Place the olive and peanut oil in a screw-top jar.

3 Replace the lid and shake well.

COOK'S TIP
Liquid dressings that contain extra-virgin olive oil should be stored at room temperature. Refrigeration can cause them to solidify.

Avocado, Crab, and Cilantro Salad

The sweet richness of crab combines especially well with ripe avocado, fresh cilantro, and tomato.

Serves 4

INGREDIENTS
1½ lb small new potatoes
1 sprig fresh mint
2 lb boiled crabs, or 10 oz frozen
    crabmeat
1 Batavia or Bibb lettuce
6 oz lamb's lettuce or young spinach
1 large ripe avocado, peeled and
    sliced
6 oz cherry tomatoes
salt, pepper and nutmeg

DRESSING
5 tbsp olive oil, preferably Tuscan
1 tbsp lime juice
3 tbsp chopped fresh cilantro
½ tsp superfine sugar

1 Scrape or peel the potatoes. Cover with water, add a good pinch of salt, and a sprig of mint. Bring to a boil and simmer for 20 minutes. Drain, cover, and keep warm until needed.

2 Remove the legs and claws from each crab. Crack these open with the back of a chopping knife and then remove the white meat.

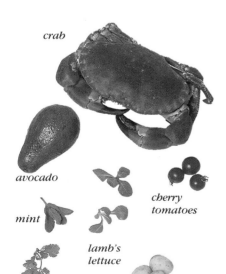

crab

avocado

mint

cherry tomatoes

lamb's lettuce

cilantro

new potatoes

3 Turn the crab on its back and push the rear leg section away with the thumb and forefinger of each hand. Remove the flesh from inside the shell.

4 Discard the soft gills ('dead men's fingers'): the crab uses these gills to filter impurities in its diet. Apart from these and the shell, everything else is edible – white and dark meat.

5 Split the central body section open with a knife and remove the white and dark flesh with a pick or skewer.

COOK'S TIP

Young crabs offer the sweetest meat, but are more difficult to prepare than older, larger ones. The female crab carries more flesh than the male, which is considered to have a better overall flavor. The male crab, shown here, is identified by his narrow apron flap at the rear. The female has a broad flap under which she carries her eggs. Frozen crabmeat is a good alternative to fresh and retains much of its original sweetness.

6 Combine the dressing ingredients in a screw-top jar and shake. Wash and spin the lettuces, then dress them. Distribute between 4 plates. Top with avocado, crab, tomatoes, and warm new potatoes. Season with salt, pepper, and freshly grated nutmeg and serve.

Swiss Cheese, Chicken, and Tongue Salad with Apple and Celery

The rich sweet flavors of this salad marry well with the tart peppery nature of watercress. A minted lemon dressing combines to freshen the overall effect. Serve with warm new potatoes.

Serves 4

INGREDIENTS
2 free-range chicken breasts, skin and
   bone removed
½ chicken stock cube
½ lb sliced tongue or ham, ¼ in thick
½ lb Swiss cheese
1 lollo rosso lettuce
1 butterhead, Batavian, or Boston
   lettuce
1 bunch watercress
2 green apples, cored and sliced
3 stalks celery, sliced
4 tbsp sesame seeds, toasted
salt, pepper, and nutmeg

DRESSING
5 tbsp peanut or sunflower oil
1 tsp sesame oil
3 tbsp lemon juice
2 tsp chopped fresh mint
3 drops Tabasco sauce

2 To make the dressing, measure the two oils, lemon juice, mint, and Tabasco sauce into a screw-top jar and shake. Cut the chicken, tongue, and cheese into fine strips. Toss with a little dressing and set aside.

3 Wash and spin the salad leaves, combine with the apple and celery, and dress. Distribute between 4 large plates. Pile the chicken, tongue, and cheese in the center, scatter with toasted sesame seeds, season with salt, pepper and freshly grated nutmeg, and serve.

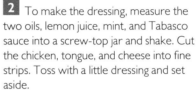

1 Place the chicken breasts in a shallow saucepan, cover with 10 fl oz water, add the ½ stock cube, and bring to a boil. Put the lid on the pan and simmer for 15 minutes. Drain, reserving the stock for another occasion, then cool the chicken under cold running water.

tongue

celery

lollo rosso lettuce

butterhead lettuce

chicken breasts

Swiss cheese

watercress

Chicken Liver, Bacon, and Tomato Salad

Warm salads are especially welcome during the autumn months when the evenings are growing shorter and cooler. Try this rich salad with sweet spinach and bitter leaves of frisée lettuce.

Serves 4

INGREDIENTS

½ lb young spinach, stems removed
1 frisée lettuce
7 tbsp peanut or sunflower oil
6 oz bacon, rind removed and cut into strips
3 slices day-old bread, crusts removed and cut into short fingers
1 lb chicken livers
4 oz cherry tomatoes
salt and pepper

2 To make the croutons, fry the bread in the bacon-flavored oil, tossing until crisp and golden. Drain on paper towels.

3 Heat the remaining 3 tbsp of oil in the skillet, add the chicken livers, and fry briskly for 2–3 minutes. Transfer the livers to the salad leaves, add the bacon, croutons, and tomatoes. Season, toss, and serve.

1 Wash and spin the salad leaves. Place in a salad bowl. Heat 4 tbsp of the oil in a large skillet. Add the bacon and cook for 3–4 minutes or until crisp and brown. Remove the bacon with a slotted spoon and drain on a piece of paper towel.

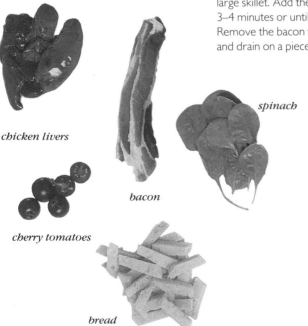

chicken livers

spinach

bacon

cherry tomatoes

bread

Maryland Salad

Barbecued chicken, sweet corn, bacon, banana, and watercress combine here in a sensational main-course salad that is out of the ordinary. Serve with baked potatoes and a knob of butter.

Serves 4

INGREDIENTS
4 boneless free-range chicken breasts
salt and pepper
½ lb bacon, rind removed
4 sweet corn cobs
3 tbsp soft butter
4 ripe bananas, peeled and halved
4 firm tomatoes, halved
1 escarole or Boston lettuce
1 bunch watercress

DRESSING
5 tbsp peanut oil
1 tbsp white-wine vinegar
2 tsp maple syrup
2 tsp mild mustard

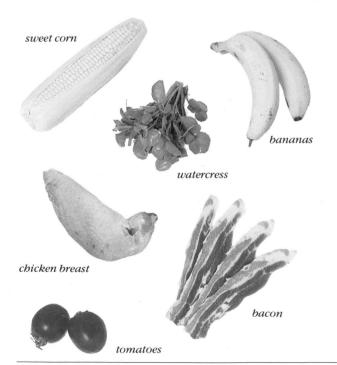

sweet corn

bananas

watercress

chicken breast

bacon

tomatoes

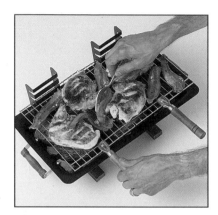

1 Season the chicken breasts, brush with oil, and barbecue or broil for 15 minutes, turning once. Barbecue or grill the bacon for 8–10 minutes or until crisp.

2 Bring a large saucepan of salted water to the boil. Shuck and trim the corn cobs or leave the husks on if you prefer. Boil for 20 minutes. For extra flavor, brush with butter and brown over the barbecue or under the broiler. Barbecue or broil the bananas and tomatoes for 6–8 minutes: you can brush these with butter too if you wish.

3 To make the dressing, combine the oil, vinegar, maple syrup, and mustard with 1 tbsp water in a screw-top jar and shake well.

4 Wash, spin thoroughly, and dress the salad leaves.

5 Distribute the salad leaves between 4 large plates. Slice the chicken and arrange over the leaves with the bacon, banana, sweet corn, and tomatoes.

Warm Pasta Salad with Ham, Egg, and Asparagus

In the summer months when the weather is hot, try serving your pasta *calda*, as a warm salad. Here it is served with ham, eggs, and asparagus. A mustard dressing made from the thick part of asparagus provides a rich accompaniment.

Serves 4

INGREDIENTS
1 lb asparagus
salt
1 lb dried tagliatelle
½ lb sliced cooked ham,
    ¼ in thick, cut into fingers
2 eggs, hard-cooked and sliced
2 oz Parmesan cheese, shaved

DRESSING
2 oz cooked potato
5 tbsp olive oil, preferably Sicilian
1 tbsp lemon juice
2 tsp Dijon mustard
½ cup vegetable stock

asparagus

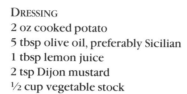

tagliatelle

Parmesan cheese

eggs

ham

1 Bring a saucepan of salted water to the boil. Trim and discard the tough woody part of the asparagus. Cut the asparagus in half and boil the thicker halves for 12 minutes. After 6 minutes throw in the tips. Refresh under cold water until warm, then drain.

2 Finely chop 5 oz of the asparagus middle section. Place in a food processor with the dressing ingredients and process until smooth. Season to taste.

3 Boil the pasta in a large saucepan of salted water according to the packet instructions. Refresh under cold water until warm, and drain. Dress with the asparagus sauce and transfer to 4 pasta plates. Top with the ham, hard-cooked eggs, and asparagus tips. Finish with Parmesan cheese.

Minted Egg and Fennel Tabbouleh with Toasted Hazelnuts

Tabbouleh, a Middle Eastern dish of steamed bulghur wheat, is suited to warm-weather picnics.

Serves 4

INGREDIENTS
1¼ cups bulghur wheat
2 eggs
1 bulb fennel
1 bunch scallions, chopped
1 oz sun-dried tomatoes, sliced
3 tbsp chopped fresh parsley
2 tbsp chopped fresh mint
3 oz black olives
4 tbsp olive oil, preferably Greek or
  Spanish
2 tbsp garlic oil (see Introduction)
2 tbsp lemon juice
salt and pepper
1 romaine lettuce
about 1 cup chopped hazelnuts,
  toasted
1 medium open-textured loaf or 4 pita
  breads, warmed

romaine lettuce

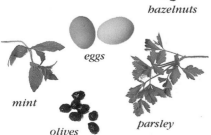
hazelnuts
eggs
mint
olives

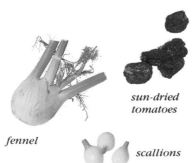
parsley
fennel
scallions
sun-dried tomatoes

1 Cover the bulghur wheat with boiling water and leave to soak for 15 minutes. Transfer to a metal strainer, position over a saucepan of boiling water, cover, and steam for 10 minutes. Spread out on a metal tray and leave to cool.

COOK'S TIP
A popular way to eat tabbouleh is to shovel it into pockets of pita bread.

2 Boil the eggs for 12 minutes. Cool under running water, shell, and quarter. Halve and finely slice the fennel. Boil in salted water for 6 minutes, drain, and cool under running water. Combine the eggs, fennel, scallions, sun-dried tomatoes, parsley, mint, and olives with the bulghur wheat. Dress with olive oil, garlic oil, and lemon juice. Season well.

3 Wash the lettuce leaves and spin dry. Line an attractive salad bowl or plate with the leaves, pile in the tabbouleh, and scatter with toasted hazelnuts. Serve with a basket of warm bread.

Goat Cheese Salad with Buckwheat, Fresh Figs, and Walnuts

The robust flavors of goat cheese and buckwheat combine especially well with ripe figs and walnuts. The olive and nut oil dressing contains no vinegar and depends instead on the acidity of the cheese. Enjoy with a gutsy red wine from either the Rhône valley or South of France.

Serves 4

INGREDIENTS

¾ cup couscous
2 tbsp toasted buckwheat
1 egg, hard-cooked
2 tbsp chopped fresh parsley
4 tbsp olive oil, preferably Sicilian
3 tbsp walnut oil
4 oz arugula
½ frisée lettuce
about 1 cup crumbly white goat
    cheese
½ cup broken walnuts, toasted
4 ripe figs, trimmed and almost cut
    into four (leave the pieces joined at
    the base)

2 Shell the hard-cooked egg and pass it through a fine grater.

3 Toss the egg, parsley, and couscous in a bowl. Combine the two oils and use half to moisten the couscous mixture.

1 Place the couscous and buckwheat in a bowl, cover with boiling water, and leave to soak for 15 minutes. Place in a strainer if necessary to drain off any remaining water, then spread out on a metal tray and allow to cool.

4 Wash and spin the salad leaves, dress with the remaining oil, and distribute between 4 large plates.

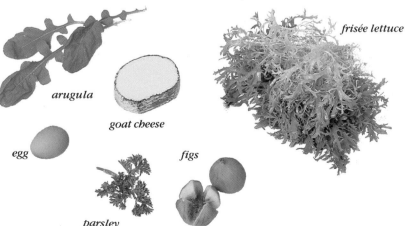

arugula

goat cheese

frisée lettuce

egg

figs

parsley

COOK'S TIP

Goat cheeses vary in strength from the youngest, which are soft and mild, to strongly flavored mature cheeses, that have a firm and crumbly texture. Crumbly cheeses are best for salads.

5 Pile the couscous in the center, crumble on the goat cheese, scatter with toasted walnuts, and add the figs.

Sweet Potato, Egg, Pork, and Beet Salad

A delicious way to use up leftover pork roast. Sweet flavors balance well with the bitterness of the salad leaves.

Serves 4

INGREDIENTS
2 lb sweet potato, peeled and diced
salt
4 heads Belgian endive
5 eggs, hard-cooked
1 lb pickled young beets
6 oz cold pork roast, sliced

DRESSING
5 tbsp peanut or sunflower oil
2 tbsp white-wine vinegar
2 tsp Dijon mustard
1 tsp fennel seeds, crushed

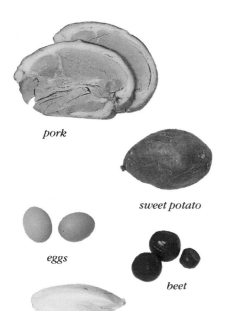

pork

sweet potato

eggs

beet

Belgian endive

1 Bring the sweet potato to a boil in salted water and cook for 10–15 minutes or until soft. Drain and allow to cool.

2 To make the dressing, combine the oil, vinegar, mustard, and fennel seeds in a screw-top jar and shake.

3 Separate the Belgian endive leaves and arrange around the edge of 4 serving plates.

4 Dress the sweet potato and spoon over the salad leaves.

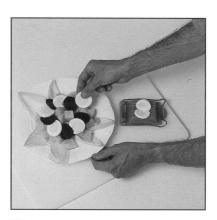

5 Shell the hard-cooked eggs. Slice the eggs and beets, and arrange to make an attractive border.

6 Cut the pork into 1½ in fingers, toss with dressing, and pile into the center. Season and serve.

Frankfurter Salad with Mustard and Caraway Dressing

A last-minute salad you can throw together using ingredients from the pantry.

Serves 4

INGREDIENTS
1 ½ lb small new potatoes, scrubbed
    or scraped
2 eggs
12 oz frankfurters
1 butterhead or Batavia lettuce
½ lb young spinach, stems removed

DRESSING
salt and pepper
3 tbsp safflower oil
2 tbsp olive oil, preferably Spanish
1 tbsp white-wine vinegar
2 tsp mustard
1 tsp caraway seeds, crushed

1 Bring the potatoes to a boil in salted water and simmer for 20 minutes. Drain, cover, and keep warm. Boil the eggs for 12 minutes. Refresh in cold water, shell, and cut into quarters.

2 Score the frankfurter skins cork-screw fashion with a small knife, then cover with boiling water and simmer for about 5 minutes to heat through. Drain well, cover, and keep warm.

butterhead lettuce

eggs

frankfurters

spinach

new potatoes

3 Combine the dressing ingredients in a screw-top jar and shake.

4 Wash and spin the salad leaves, toss with half of the dressing, and distribute between 4 large plates.

5 Toss the potatoes and frankfurters with the remainder of the dressing, and scatter over the salad.

6 Finish with sections of hard-cooked egg, season, and serve.

COOK'S TIP

Mustard has an important place in the salad maker's pantry. Varieties differ from country to country and often suggest particular flavors. This salad has a German slant to it and calls for a sweet and sour German-style mustard. American mustards have a similar quality.

Pear and Pecan Salad with Blue Cheese Dressing

Toasted pecans have a special affinity for crisp white pears. Their robust flavors combine especially well with a rich blue cheese dressing and make this a salad to remember.

Serves 4

INGREDIENTS
½ cup shelled pecans, roughly chopped
3 crisp pears
6 oz young spinach, stems removed
1 escarole or Boston lettuce
1 radicchio
2 tbsp Blue Cheese and Chive Dressing
salt and pepper
crusty bread, to serve

1 Toast the pecans under a moderate broiler to bring out their flavor.

2 Cut the pears into even slices, leaving the skin intact, and discarding the cores.

3 Wash the salad leaves and spin dry. Add the pears together with the toasted pecans, then toss with the dressing. Distribute between 4 large plates and season with salt and pepper. Serve with warm crusty bread.

escarole

pears

pecans

radicchio

spinach

Warm Fish Salad with Mango Dressing

This salad is best served during the summer months, preferably outdoors. The dressing combines the flavor of rich mango with hot chili, ginger, and lime.

Serves 4

INGREDIENTS
1 French bread
4 redfish, black bream or porgy, each
   weighing about 10 oz
1 tbsp vegetable oil
1 mango
½ in fresh ginger
1 fresh red chili, seeded and finely
   chopped
2 tbsp lime juice
2 tbsp chopped fresh cilantro
6 oz young spinach
5 oz bok choy
6 oz cherry tomatoes, halved

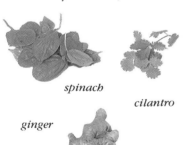

spinach

cilantro

ginger

porgy

cherry tomatoes

mango

I Preheat the oven to 350°F. Cut the French bread into 8 in lengths. Slice lengthwise, then cut into thick fingers. Place the bread on a baking sheet and dry in the oven for 15 minutes. Preheat the broiler or light the barbecue and allow the embers to settle. Score the fish deeply on both sides and moisten with oil. Broil or barbecue for about 6 minutes, turning once.

2 Place one half of the mango flesh in a food processor. Peel the ginger, grate finely, then add with the chili, lime juice, and cilantro. Process until smooth. Adjust to a pouring consistency with 2–3 tbsp water if necessary.

3 Wash the salad leaves and spin dry, then distribute them between 4 plates. Place the fish over the leaves. Spoon on the mango dressing and finish with slices of mango and tomato halves. Serve with fingers of crispy French bread.

COOK'S TIP

Other varieties of fish suitable for this salad include salmon, monkfish, tuna, sea bass, and halibut.

Grilled Salmon and Spring Vegetable Salad

Spring is the time to enjoy sweet young vegetables. Cook them briefly, cool to room temperature, dress, and serve with a piece of lightly grilled salmon topped with sorrel and quail's eggs.

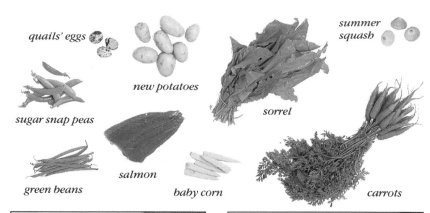

quails' eggs

summer squash

new potatoes

sorrel

sugar snap peas

green beans

salmon

baby corn

carrots

Serves 4

INGREDIENTS

12 oz small new potatoes, scrubbed or scraped
salt and pepper
4 quails' eggs
¼ lb young carrots, peeled
¼ lb baby corn
¼ lb sugar snap peas, trimmed and stringed
¼ lb fine green beans, trimmed and stringed
¼ lb young zucchini
¼ lb summer squash (optional)

½ cup French Dressing
4 salmon fillets, each weighing 5 oz, skinned
¼ lb sorrel or young spinach, stems removed

1 Bring the potatoes to a boil in salted water and cook for 15–20 minutes. Drain, cover, and keep warm.

2 Cover the quails' eggs with boiling water and cook for 8 minutes. Refresh under cold water, shell, and cut in half.

3 Bring a saucepan of salted water to a boil, add all the vegetables, and cook for 2–3 minutes. Drain well. Place the hot vegetables and potatoes in a bowl, toss with French Dressing, and allow to cool.

4 Brush the salmon fillets with French Dressing and broil for about 6 minutes, turning once.

5 Place the sorrel in a stainless steel or enamel saucepan with 2 tbsp French Dressing, cover, and soften over a gentle heat for 2 minutes. Strain, then allow to cool to room temperature. Toss the vegetables in the remaining French Dressing.

6 Divide the potatoes and vegetables between 4 large plates, then position a piece of salmon to one side of each. Finally place a spoonful of sorrel on each piece of salmon and top with a halved quail's egg. Season and serve at room temperature.

Salade Mouclade

Mouclade is a long-established dish from La Rochelle in southwestern France. The dish consists of mussels in a light curry cream sauce and is usually served hot. Here the flavors appear in a salad of warm lentils and lightly cooked spinach. Serve at room temperature during the summer months.

Serves 4

INGREDIENTS

3 tbsp olive oil, preferably French or
  Italian
1 medium onion, finely chopped
1¾ cups Puy or green lentils, soaked
  for 2 hours
3¾ cups vegetable stock
4½ lb fresh mussels in their shells
5 tbsp white wine
½ tsp mild curry paste
1 pinch saffron
2 tbsp heavy cream
salt and cayenne pepper
2 large carrots, peeled
4 stalks celery
2 lb young spinach, stems removed
1 tbsp garlic oil (see Introduction)

carrot

onion

celery

green lentils   *mussels*

1 Heat the oil in a heavy saucepan and soften the onion for 6–8 minutes. Add the drained lentils and vegetable stock, bring to a boil, and simmer for 45 minutes. Remove from the heat and cool.

2 Clean the mussels thoroughly, discarding any that are damaged. Any that are open should close if given a sharp tap; if they fail to do so, discard these too. Place the mussels in a large saucepan, add the wine, cover, and steam over a high heat for 12 minutes. Strain the mussels in a colander, collecting the cooking liquor in a bowl, and discard any that have not opened during cooking. Allow the mussels to cool, then take them out of their shells.

3 Pass the mussel liquor through a fine strainer or cheesecloth into a wide shallow saucepan to remove any grit or sand. Add the curry paste and saffron, then reduce over a high heat until almost dry. Remove from the heat, stir in the cream, season, and combine with the mussels.

4 Bring a saucepan of salted water to a boil. Cut the carrot and celery into 2 in matchsticks, cook for 3 minutes, drain, cool, and drizzle with olive oil.

5 Wash the spinach, put the wet leaves into a large saucepan, cover, and steam for 30 seconds. Immerse in cold water and press the leaves dry with the back of a large spoon in a colander. Toss with garlic oil, season, and set aside.

6 Spoon the lentils into the center of 4 large plates. Place 5 heaps of spinach around the edge of each one and position some carrot and celery on top of each heap. Spoon the mussels over the lentils and serve at room temperature.

CLASSIC SALADS

Salade Niçoise

Salade Niçoise is the happy marriage of tuna fish, hard-cooked eggs, green beans, and potatoes. Anchovies, olives, and capers are often also included, but it is the first four ingredients that combine to make this a classic salad.

Serves 4

INGREDIENTS
1½ lb potatoes, peeled
salt and pepper
½ lb green beans, trimmed and
    stringed
3 eggs, hard-cooked
1 romaine lettuce
½ cup French Dressing
½ lb small plum tomatoes, quartered
14 oz canned albacore tuna in oil,
    drained
1 oz canned anchovies
2 tbsp capers
12 black olives

2 Slice the potatoes thickly. Shell and quarter the eggs.

3 Wash the lettuce and spin dry, then chop the leaves roughly. Toss with half of the dressing in a large salad bowl.

1 Bring the potatoes to a boil in salted water and cook for 20 minutes. Boil the green beans for 6 minutes. Drain and cool the potatoes and beans under running water.

romaine lettuce

green beans

olives

potatoes

anchovies

plum tomatoes

capers

4 Toss the potatoes, green beans, and tomatoes with dressing, then scatter over the salad leaves.

COOK'S TIP

The ingredients for Salade Niçoise can be prepared well in advance and should be assembled just before serving to retain flavor and freshness.

5 Break the tuna fish up with a fork and distribute over the salad with the anchovies, capers, and olives. Season to taste and serve.

Ratatouille

Ratatouille is a combination of tomatoes, onions, peppers, eggplants, and zucchini cooked in olive oil and garlic. This Mediterranean dish is often served at room temperature during summer months and is delicious with a salad of white beans, a few anchovies, and a basket of crispy bread.

Serves 4

INGREDIENTS
6 small eggplants
1 large onion, roughly chopped
3 cloves garlic, crushed
²⁄₃ cup olive oil, preferably French or Spanish
½ lb zucchini, thickly sliced
1 large green bell pepper, seeded and roughly chopped
12 oz ripe tomatoes, peeled and quartered
2 tsp olive paste (optional)
2 tbsp red-wine vinegar
5 tbsp chopped fresh herbs: parsley, basil, tarragon, oregano
salt and pepper

1 Halve the eggplants, then slice thickly. If the eggplants are large, you will need to extract the bitter juices. To do this, sprinkle the cut surfaces generously with salt and secure between 2 large plates. After 20 minutes a clear liquid will emerge. Rinse well in cold water to remove the salt and dry well.

2 Soften the onion and garlic in olive oil for 6–8 minutes. Add the eggplant, zucchini, green bell pepper, tomatoes, and olive paste (if using). Simmer, uncovered, for 40 minutes.

3 To finish, stir in the vinegar and herbs. Season to taste and allow to cool.

parsley

tomatoes

bell pepper

eggplants

oregano

basil

zucchini

garlic

Waldorf Ham Salad

Waldorf salad first appeared at the Waldorf Astoria Hotel, New York, in the 1890s. Originally it consisted of apples, celery, and mayonnaise. It was commonly served with duck, ham, and goose. This modern-day version often includes meat and is something of a meal in itself.

Serves 4

INGREDIENTS

3 apples, peeled
1 tbsp lemon juice
2 slices cooked ham, each weighing
   6 oz
3 stalks celery
⅔ cup mayonnaise
1 escarole or Batavia lettuce
1 small radicchio, finely shredded
½ bunch watercress
3 tbsp walnut oil or olive oil
½ cup walnut pieces, toasted
salt and pepper

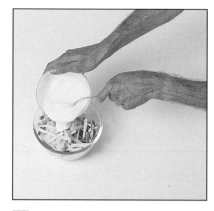

2 Add the mayonnaise to the apples, ham, and celery and mix well.

3 Wash and spin the salad leaves. Shred the leaves finely, then toss with walnut oil. Distribute the leaves between 4 plates. Pile the mayonnaise mixture in the center, scatter with toasted walnuts, season, and serve.

1 Core, slice, and shred the apples finely. Moisten with lemon juice to keep them white. Cut the ham into 2 in strips, then cut the celery into similar-sized pieces, and combine in a bowl.

apple

watercress

celery

walnuts

radicchio

escarole

Caesar Salad

There are many stories about the origin of Caesar Salad. The most likely is that it was invented by an Italian, Caesar Cardini, who owned a restaurant in Mexico in the 1920s. Simplicity is the key to its success.

Serves 4

INGREDIENTS
3 slices day-old bread, ½ in thick
4 tbsp garlic oil (see Introduction)
salt and pepper
2 oz piece Parmesan cheese
1 romaine lettuce

DRESSING
2 egg yolks, as fresh as possible
1 oz canned anchovies, roughly
    chopped
½ tsp Dijon mustard
½ cup olive oil, preferably Italian
1 tbsp white-wine vinegar

COOK'S TIP

The classic dressing for Caesar Salad is made with raw egg yolks. Ensure you use only the freshest eggs, bought from a reputable dealer. Expectant mothers, young children and the elderly are not advised to eat raw egg yolks. You could omit them from the dressing and grate hard-cooked yolks on top of the salad instead.

1 To make the dressing, combine the egg yolks, anchovies, mustard, oil, and vinegar in a screw-top jar and shake well.

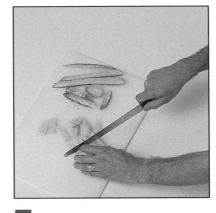

2 Remove the crusts from the bread with a serrated knife and cut into 1 in fingers.

3 Heat the garlic oil in a large skillet, add the pieces of bread, and fry until golden. Sprinkle with salt and leave to drain on paper towels.

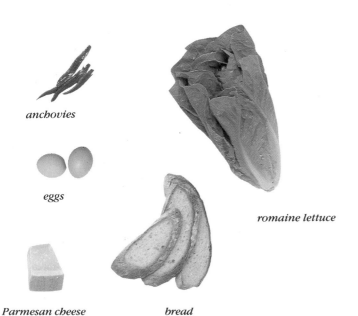

anchovies

eggs

romaine lettuce

Parmesan cheese　*bread*

4 Cut thin shavings from the Parmesan cheese with a vegetable peeler.

5 Wash the salad leaves and spin dry. Smother with the dressing, and scatter with garlic croutons and Parmesan cheese. Season and serve.

Gado Gado

Gado Gado is a traditional Indonesian salad around which friends and family gather to eat. Fillings are chosen and wrapped in a lettuce leaf. The parcel is then dipped in a spicy peanut sauce and eaten. Salad ingredients vary according to what is in season.

Serves 4

INGREDIENTS

2 medium potatoes, peeled
salt
3 eggs
6 oz green beans, trimmed and
   stringed
1 romaine lettuce
4 tomatoes, cut into wedges
¼ lb bean sprouts
½ hothouse cucumber, peeled and
   cut into fingers
5 oz giant white radish (mooli),
   peeled and grated
6 oz tofu, cut into large dice
12 oz large cooked peeled shrimp
1 small bunch fresh cilantro

SPICY PEANUT SAUCE

5 oz/½ cup smooth peanut butter
juice of ½ lemon
2 shallots or 1 small onion, finely
   chopped
1 clove garlic, crushed
1–2 small fresh red chilies, seeded and
   finely chopped
2 tbsp southeast Asian fish sauce
   (optional)
⅔ cup coconut milk, canned or fresh
1 tbsp superfine sugar

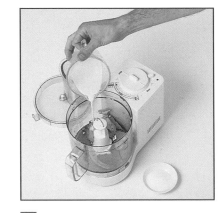

1 To make the Spicy Peanut Sauce, combine the ingredients in a food processor until smooth.

cilantro

potatoes

shrimp

romaine lettuce

green beans

cucumber

eggs

bean sprouts

giant white radish (mooli)

2 Bring the potatoes to a boil in salted water and simmer for 20 minutes. Bring a second pan of salted water to a boil. To save using too many pans, cook the eggs and beans together: lower the eggs into the boiling water in the second pan; then, after 6 minutes, add the beans and boil for a further 6 minutes. (Hard-cooked eggs should have a total of 12 minutes.) Cool the potatoes, eggs, and beans under running water.

3 Line a large platter with the outer leaves of the lettuce. Pile the remainder to one side of the platter.

4 Slice the potatoes. Shell and quarter the eggs. Arrange the potatoes, eggs, beans, and tomatoes in separate piles. Arrange the other salad ingredients in a similar way to cover the platter.

HANDLING CHILIES

Red chilies are considered to be sweeter and hotter than green ones. Smaller varieties of both red and green are likely to be more pungent than large varieties. You can lessen the intensity of a fresh chili by splitting it open and removing the white seed-bearing membrane. The residue given off when chilies are cut can cause serious burns to the skin. Be sure to wash your hands thoroughly after handling raw chilies and avoid touching your eyes or any sensitive skin areas.

5 Transfer the Spicy Peanut Sauce into an attractive bowl and bring to the table with the salad.

Poor Boy Steak Salad

'Poor Boy' started life in the Italian Creole community of New Orleans when the poor survived on sandwiches filled with leftover scraps. Times have improved since then, and today the 'Poor Boy' sandwich is commonly filled with tender beef strips and other goodies. This is a salad version of 'Poor Boy'.

Serves 4

INGREDIENTS
4 sirloin or rump steaks, each
    weighing 6 oz
1 escarole lettuce
1 bunch watercress
4 tomatoes, quartered
4 large dill pickles, sliced
4 scallions, sliced
4 canned artichoke hearts, halved
6 oz button mushrooms, sliced
12 green olives
½ cup French Dressing
salt and black pepper

1 Season the steaks with black pepper. Cook the steaks under a moderate broiler for 6–8 minutes, turning once, until medium-rare. Cover and leave to rest in a warm place.

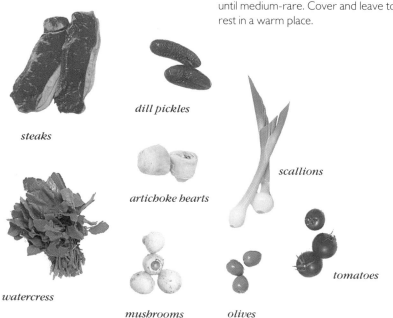

steaks

dill pickles

artichoke hearts

scallions

watercress

mushrooms

olives

tomatoes

2 Wash the salad leaves and spin dry. Combine with the remainder of the ingredients (except the steak) and toss with the French Dressing.

3 Divide the salad between 4 plates. Slice each steak diagonally and position over the salad. Season with salt and serve.

Russian Salad

Russian salad became fashionable in the hotel dining rooms of Europe in the 1920s and 1930s. Originally it consisted of lightly cooked vegetables, eggs, shellfish, and mayonnaise. Today we find it diced in plastic tubs in supermarkets. This version recalls better days and plays on the theme of the Fabergé egg.

Serves 4

INGREDIENTS
¼ lb large button mushrooms
½ cup mayonnaise
1 tbsp lemon juice
12 oz cooked peeled shrimp
1 large dill pickle, chopped, or 2 tbsp capers
salt, pepper, and paprika
¼ lb fava beans
¼ lb small new potatoes, scrubbed or scraped
¼ lb young carrots, trimmed and peeled
¼ lb baby corn
¼ lb baby turnips, trimmed
1 tbsp olive oil, preferably French or Italian
4 eggs, hard-cooked and shelled
1 oz canned anchovies, cut into fine strips

1 Slice the mushrooms thinly, then cut into matchsticks. Combine the mayonnaise and lemon juice. Fold half of the mayonnaise into the mushrooms and shrimp, add the chopped dill pickle, then season to taste.

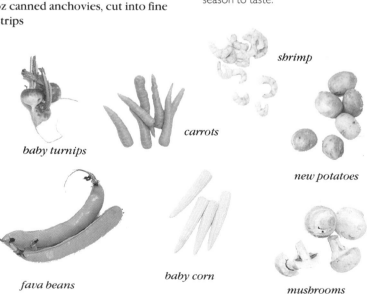

shrimp

carrots

baby turnips

new potatoes

fava beans

baby corn

mushrooms

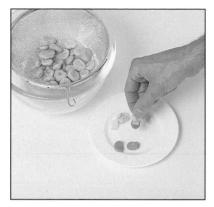

2 Bring a large saucepan of salted water to a boil, add the fava beans, and cook for 3 minutes. Drain and cool under running water, then pinch the beans between thumb and forefinger to release them from their tough skins. Boil the potatoes for 20 minutes and the remaining vegetables for 6 minutes. Drain and cool under running water.

3 Toss the vegetables with oil and divide between 4 shallow bowls. Spoon on the dressed shrimp and place a hard-cooked egg in the center. Decorate the egg with strips of anchovy and sprinkle with paprika.

San Francisco Salad

California is a salad maker's paradise and is renowned for the healthiness of its produce. San Francisco has become the salad capital of California, although this recipe is based on a salad served at the Chez Panisse restaurant in Berkeley.

Serves 4

INGREDIENTS
2 lb langoustines, or jumbo shrimp
salt and cayenne pepper
2 oz bulb fennel, sliced
2 ripe medium tomatoes, quartered, and 4 small tomatoes
2 tbsp olive oil, plus extra for tossing the salad leaves
4 tbsp brandy
⅔ cup dry white wine
7 fl oz can lobster or crab bisque
2 tbsp chopped fresh tarragon
3 tbsp heavy cream
8 oz green beans, trimmed and stringed
2 oranges
6 oz lamb's lettuce
¼ lb arugula
½ frisée lettuce

frisée lettuce

langoustines

tomatoes   *fennel*   *orange*

lamb's lettuce

arugula

1 Bring a large saucepan of salted water to a boil, add the langoustines (or shrimp), and simmer for 10 minutes. Refresh under cold running water.

2 Preheat the oven to 425°F. Twist the tails from all but 4 of the langoustines (or peel and devein the shrimp): reserve these to garnish the dish. Peel the outer shell from the tail. Put the tail peelings, carapace and claws in a roasting pan with the fennel and tomatoes. Toss with 2 tbsp oil and roast near the top of the oven for 20 minutes.

3 Remove the roasting pan from the oven and place it over a moderate heat on top of the stove. Add the brandy and ignite to release the flavor of the alcohol. Add the wine and simmer briefly.

4 Transfer the contents of the roasting pan to a food processor and process until coarse: this will take only 10–15 seconds. Force through a fine nylon strainer into a bowl. Add the lobster bisque, tarragon, and cream. Season to taste with salt and a little cayenne pepper. Wash and spin the salad leaves. Set aside.

5 Bring a saucepan of salted water to a boil and cook the beans for 6 minutes. Drain and cool under running water. To segment the oranges, cut the peel from the top and bottom, and then from the sides, with a serrated knife. Loosen the segments by cutting between the membranes and the flesh.

6 Toss the lettuce with olive oil and distribute between 4 serving plates. Fold the langoustine or shrimp into the dressing and distribute between the plates. Add the beans, oranges, and small tomatoes, decorate each with a whole langoustine (or shrimp) and serve warm.

Shrimp Salad with Curry Dressing

Curry spices add an unexpected twist to this salad. Warm flavors combine especially well with sweet shrimp and grated apple.

Serves 4

INGREDIENTS
1 ripe tomato
½ iceberg lettuce, shredded
1 small onion
1 small bunch fresh cilantro
1 tbsp lemon juice
salt
1 lb cooked peeled shrimp
1 apple, peeled

DRESSING
5 tbsp mayonnaise
1 tsp mild curry paste
1 tbsp tomato ketchup

TO DECORATE
8 whole shrimp
8 lemon wedges
4 sprigs fresh cilantro

1 To peel the tomato, pierce the skin with a knife and immerse in boiling water for 20 seconds. Drain and cool under running water. Peel off the skin. Halve the tomato, push the seeds out with your thumb, and discard them. Cut the flesh into a large dice.

shrimp *cilantro* *tomato* *apple* *lemon* *onion*

2 Finely shred the lettuce, onion, and cilantro. Add the tomato, toss with lemon juice, and season with salt.

3 To make the dressing, combine the mayonnaise, curry paste, and tomato ketchup in a small bowl. Add 2 tbsp water to thin the dressing and season to taste with salt.

4 Combine the shrimp with the dressing. Quarter and core the apple, and grate into the mixture.

COOK'S TIP

Fresh cilantro is inclined to wilt if kept out of water. Keep it in a jar of water in the refrigerator covered with a plastic bag and it will stay fresh for several days.

5 Distribute the shredded lettuce mixture between 4 plates or bowls. Pile the shrimp mixture in the center of each and decorate with 2 whole shrimp, 2 lemon wedges, and a sprig of cilantro.

Apple Coleslaw

The term coleslaw stems from the Dutch *koolsla*, meaning 'cool cabbage'. There are many variations of this salad; this recipe combines the sweet flavors of apple and carrot with celery salt. Coleslaw is traditionally served with cold ham.

Serves 4

INGREDIENTS
1 lb white cabbage
1 medium onion
2 apples, peeled and cored
6 oz carrots, peeled
²⁄₃ cup mayonnaise
1 tsp celery salt
black pepper

carrots

onion

apple

white cabbage

2 Feed the cabbage and the onion through a food processor fitted with a slicing blade. Change to a grating blade and grate the apples and carrots. Alternatively, use a hand grater and vegetable slicer.

3 Combine the salad ingredients in a large bowl. Fold in the mayonnaise and season with celery salt and freshly ground black pepper.

1 Discard the outside leaves of the cabbage if they are dirty, cut the cabbage into 2 in wedges, then remove the stem section.

Cook's Tip

This recipe can be easily adapted to suit different tastes. You could add ½ cup chopped walnuts or raisins for added texture. For a richer coleslaw, add ½ cup grated Cheddar cheese. You may find you will need smaller portions, as the cheese makes a more filling dish.

Potato Salad with Egg and Lemon Dressing

Potato salads are a popular addition to any salad spread and are enjoyed with an assortment of cold meats and fish. This recipe draws on the contrasting flavors of egg and lemon. Chopped parsley provides a fresh finish.

Serves 4

INGREDIENTS
2 lb new potatoes, scrubbed or
   scraped
salt and pepper
1 medium onion, finely chopped
1 egg, hard-cooked
1¼ cups mayonnaise
1 clove garlic, crushed
finely grated zest and juice of 1 lemon
4 tbsp chopped fresh parsley

COOK'S TIP

At certain times of the year potatoes are inclined to fall apart when boiled. This usually coincides with the end of a particular season when potatoes become starchy. Early-season varieties are therefore best for making salads.

egg

garlic

onion

lemon

new potatoes

1 Bring the potatoes to a boil in a saucepan of salted water. Simmer for 20 minutes. Drain and allow to cool. Cut the potatoes into large dice, season well, and combine with the onion.

2 Shell the hard-cooked egg and grate into a mixing bowl, then add the mayonnaise. Combine the garlic and lemon zest and juice in a small bowl and stir into the mayonnaise.

3 Fold in the chopped parsley, mix thoroughly into the potatoes, and serve.

Sweet Turnip Salad with Horseradish and Caraway

The robust-flavored turnip goes well with the taste of horseradish and caraway seeds. This salad is delicious with cold roast beef or smoked trout.

Serves 4

INGREDIENTS
12 oz medium turnips
2 scallions, white part only, chopped
1 tbsp superfine sugar
salt
2 tbsp prepared horseradish
2 tsp caraway seeds

turnips

COOK'S TIP
If turnips are not available, giant white radish (mooli) can be used as a substitute.

1 Peel, slice, and shred the turnips – or grate them if you wish.

2 Add the scallions, sugar, and salt, then rub together with your hands to soften the turnip.

3 Fold in the prepared horseradish and caraway seeds.

scallions

Tomato and Feta Cheese Salad

Sweet sun-ripened tomatoes are rarely more delicious than when served with feta cheese and olive oil. This salad, popular in Greece and Turkey, is enjoyed as a light meal with pieces of crispy bread.

Serves 4

INGREDIENTS
2 lb tomatoes
7 oz feta cheese
½ cup olive oil, preferably Greek
12 black olives
4 sprigs fresh basil
black pepper

COOK'S TIP

Feta cheese has a strong flavor and can be salty. The least salty variety is imported from Greece and Turkey, and is available from specialty or gourmet stores.

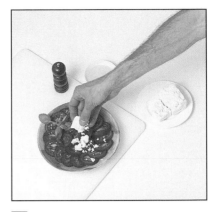

2 Slice the tomatoes thickly and arrange in a shallow dish.

3 Crumble the cheese over the tomatoes, sprinkle with olive oil, then sprinkle over the olives and fresh basil. Season with freshly ground black pepper and serve at room temperature.

I Remove the tough cores from the tomatoes with a small knife.

tomatoes

basil

feta cheese

olives

Leeks with Parsley, Egg, and Walnut Dressing

In French cooking, leeks are valued for their smooth texture as well as their flavor. They make a wonderful salad, which should be eaten slightly warm, so it is the ideal dish to serve with assorted pâtés and boiled new potatoes for a gourmet picnic feast.

Serves 4

INGREDIENTS
1½ lb young leeks
1 egg

DRESSING
1 oz fresh parsley
2 tbsp olive oil, preferably French
juice of ½ lemon
½ cup broken walnuts, toasted
1 tsp superfine sugar
salt and pepper

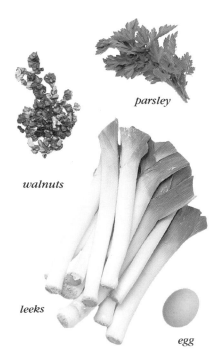

parsley

walnuts

leeks

egg

1 Bring a saucepan of salted water to a boil. Cut the leeks into 4 in lengths and rinse well to flush out any grit or soil. Cook the leeks for 8 minutes. Drain and part-cool under running water.

2 Lower the egg into boiling water and cook for 12 minutes. Cool under running water, shell, and set aside.

3 For the dressing, finely chop the parsley in a food processor.

4 Add the olive oil, lemon juice, and toasted walnuts. Blend for 1–2 minutes until smooth.

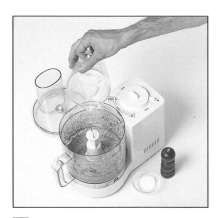

5 Adjust the consistency with about ⅓ cup water. Add the sugar and season to taste with salt and pepper.

6 Place the leeks on an attractive plate, then spoon on the sauce. Finely grate the hard-cooked egg and scatter over the sauce. Serve at room temperature.

Tzatziki

Tzatziki is a Greek cucumber salad dressed with yogurt, mint, and garlic. It is typically served with grilled lamb and chicken, but is also good with salmon and trout.

Serves 4

INGREDIENTS
1 hothouse cucumber
1 tsp salt
3 tbsp finely chopped fresh mint, plus
    a few sprigs to garnish
1 clove garlic, crushed
1 tsp superfine sugar
scant 1 cup strained thick, Greek-style
    plain yogurt
paprika, to garnish (optional)

mint

cucumber

1 Peel the cucumber. Reserve a little to use as a garnish if you wish and cut the rest in half lengthwise. Remove the seeds with a teaspoon and discard. Slice the cucumber thinly and combine with salt. Leave for approximately 15–20 minutes. Salt will soften the cucumber and draw out any bitter juices.

2 Combine the mint, garlic, sugar, and yogurt in a bowl, reserving a few sprigs of mint as decoration.

3 Rinse the cucumber in a strainer under cold running water to remove the salt. Drain well and combine with the yogurt. Decorate with cucumber and mint. Serve cold. Tzatziki is traditionally garnished with paprika.

COOK'S TIP

If preparing Tzatziki in a hurry, leave out the method for salting cucumber at the end of step 1. The cucumber will have a more crunchy texture, and will be slightly less sweet.

Green Bean Salad with Egg Topping

When green beans are fresh and plentiful, serve them lightly cooked as a light entree topped with butter-fried bread crumbs, egg, and parsley.

Serves 4

INGREDIENTS
1½ lb green beans, trimmed and
    stringed
salt
2 tbsp garlic oil (see Introduction)
1 oz butter
1 cup fresh white bread crumbs
4 tbsp chopped fresh parsley
1 egg, hard-cooked and shelled

2 Heat the butter in a large skillet, add the bread crumbs, and fry until golden. Remove from the heat, add the parsley, then grate in the hard-cooked egg.

3 Place the beans in a shallow serving dish and spoon on the bread crumb topping. Serve at room temperature.

1 Bring a large saucepan of salted water to the boil. Add the beans and cook for 6 minutes. Drain well, toss in garlic oil, and allow to cool.

parsley

egg

green beans

COOK'S TIP

Few cooks need reminding how to boil an egg, but many are faced with the problem of a dark ring around the yolk when cooked. This is caused by boiling for longer than the optimum period of 12 minutes. Allow boiled eggs to cool in water for easy peeling.

White Bean and Celery Salad

This simple bean salad is a delicious alternative to the potato salad that seems to appear at every picnic spread. If you do not have time to soak and cook dried beans, use canned ones.

Serves 4

INGREDIENTS
1 lb dried white beans (haricot, canellini, navy, or butter beans) or 3 × 14 oz cans white beans
4½ cups vegetable stock, made from a cube
3 stalks celery, cut into ½ in strips
½ cup French Dressing
3 tbsp chopped fresh parsley
salt and pepper

parsley

white beans

celery

COOK'S TIP

Dried beans that have been kept for longer than 6 months will need soaking overnight to lessen their cooking time. As a rule, the less time beans have been kept, the shorter the soaking and cooking time they need. The times given here are suited to freshly purchased beans.

2 Place the cooked beans in a large saucepan. Add the vegetable stock and celery, bring to a boil, cover, and simmer for 15 minutes. Drain thoroughly. Toss the beans with the dressing and leave to cool.

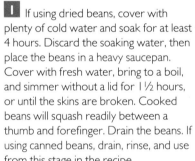

1 If using dried beans, cover with plenty of cold water and soak for at least 4 hours. Discard the soaking water, then place the beans in a heavy saucepan. Cover with fresh water, bring to a boil, and simmer without a lid for 1½ hours, or until the skins are broken. Cooked beans will squash readily between a thumb and forefinger. Drain the beans. If using canned beans, drain, rinse, and use from this stage in the recipe.

3 Add the chopped parsley and season to taste with salt and pepper.

Guacamole Salad Dip

Creamy rich guacamole is a welcome sight at any party gathering. If you are cooking a Mexican meal, serve it as a salad dip with tortilla chips, raw vegetables, and crispy potato skins.

Serves 4

INGREDIENTS
2 large ripe avocados
2 cloves garlic, crushed
1 small onion, finely chopped
4 tbsp lemon juice
1 fresh green chili, seeded and chopped (optional)
3 tbsp chopped fresh cilantro
salt
Tabasco sauce

TO SERVE
5 large potatoes
1 tbsp vegetable oil
salt
4 stalks celery, cut into fingers
3 large ripe tomatoes, cut into wedges
1 mild onion, cut into strips
tortilla chips
8 Jalapeño or soft green chilies (optional)

cilantro

chili

tomato

potatoes

celery

onion

garlic

avocado

1 Halve each avocado lengthwise, discard the pit, and scoop the flesh into a food processor.

COOK'S TIP

Choose avocados that yield to firm pressure near the stem. The fruits ripen most effectively if they are kept in a brown paper bag with ripe bananas or mangoes.

2 Add the garlic, onion, lemon juice and green chili (if using). Blend roughly. Add the cilantro and season to taste with salt and Tabasco sauce. Cover closely with plastic wrap to prevent discoloration.

3 To prepare potato skins, thickly peel the potatoes: you should aim for 6–8 large pieces of peel from each one. Cover with boiling water and cook for 5 minutes. Meanwhile preheat the broiler or barbecue to a moderate temperature. Drain the potato skins well, toss in oil, season with salt, and broil until crisp. Transfer the guacamole to an attractive bowl, place on a serving plate with the dipping ingredients, and serve.

Arugula, Pear, and Parmesan Salad

For a sophisticated start to an elaborate meal, try this simple salad of honey-rich pears, fresh Parmesan, and aromatic leaves of arugula. Enjoy with a young Beaujolais or chilled Lambrusco wine.

Serves 4

INGREDIENTS
3 ripe pears, Williams or Packhams
2 tsp lemon juice
3 tbsp hazelnut or walnut oil
4 oz arugula
3 oz Parmesan cheese
black pepper
open-textured bread, to serve

arugula

Parmesan cheese

pears

1 Peel and core the pears and slice thickly. Toss with lemon juice to keep the flesh white.

2 Combine the nut oil with the pears. Add the arugula leaves and toss.

3 Transfer the salad to 4 small plates and top with shavings of Parmesan cheese. Season with freshly ground black pepper and serve.

COOK'S TIP

If you are unable to buy arugula easily, you can grow your own from early spring to late summer.

Cachumbar

Cachumbar is a salad relish most commonly served with Indian curries. There are many versions, although this one will leave your mouth feeling cool and refreshed after a spicy meal.

Serves 4

INGREDIENTS
3 ripe tomatoes
2 scallions, chopped
¼ tsp superfine sugar
salt
3 tbsp chopped fresh cilantro

tomatoes

cilantro

scallion

COOK'S TIP
Cachumbar also makes a fine accompaniment to fresh crab, lobster, and shellfish.

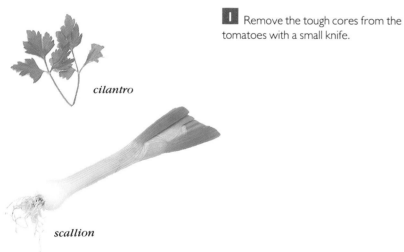

I Remove the tough cores from the tomatoes with a small knife.

2 Halve the tomatoes, remove the seeds, and dice the flesh.

3 Combine the tomatoes with the scallions, sugar, salt, and chopped cilantro. Serve at room temperature.

Exotic Thai Fish Salad

For a tropical taste of the Far East, try this delicious fish salad scented with coconut, fruit, and warm Thai spices.

Serves 4

INGREDIENTS

12 oz fillet of red mullet, sea bream, or red snapper
1 romaine lettuce
½ lollo biondo lettuce
1 papaya or mango, peeled and sliced
1 pitaya, peeled and sliced
1 large ripe tomato, cut into wedges
½ hothouse cucumber, peeled and cut into batons
3 scallions, sliced

DRESSING

1 tbsp unsweetened cream of coconut
salt
4 tbsp peanut or safflower oil
finely grated zest and juice of 1 lime
1 fresh red chili, seeded and finely chopped
1 tsp sugar
3 tbsp chopped fresh cilantro

MARINADE

1 tsp coriander seeds
1 tsp fennel seeds
½ tsp cumin seeds
1 tsp superfine sugar
½ tsp hot chili sauce
2 tbsp garlic oil (see Introduction)
salt

lollo biondo lettuce   *cucumber*

tomato

red mullet   *scallions*   *romaine lettuce*   *papaya*

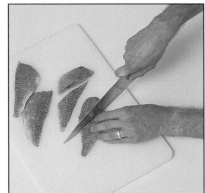

1 Cut the fish into even strips and place on a plate or in a shallow bowl.

2 For the marinade, crush the coriander, fennel, and cumin seeds with the sugar. Add the chili sauce, garlic oil, and salt and combine.

3 Spread the marinade over the fish, cover, and leave to stand in a cool place for at least 20 minutes – longer if you have time.

4 To make the dressing, place the coconut and salt in a screw-top jar with 3 tbsp boiling water. Add the oil, lime zest and juice, red chili, sugar, and chopped fresh cilantro. Shake well and set aside.

5 Wash and spin the lettuce leaves. Combine with the papaya, pitaya, tomato, cucumber, and scallions. Toss with the dressing, then distribute between 4 large plates.

6 Heat a large nonstick skillet. add the fish and cook for 5 minutes, turning once. Place the cooked fish on top of the salad and serve.

COOK'S TIP

If planning ahead, you can leave the fish in its marinade for up to 8 hours. The dressing can also be made in advance minus the fresh cilantro. Store at room temperature and add the cilantro when you are ready to assemble the salad.

Melon and Prosciutto Salad with Strawberry Salsa

Sections of cool fragrant melon wrapped with slices of air-dried ham make a delicious salad starter. If strawberries are in season, serve with a savory-sweet strawberry salsa and watch it disappear.

Serves 4

INGREDIENTS
1 large melon, cantaloupe, Spanish or
    charentais
6 oz prosciutto, thinly sliced

SALSA
½ lb strawberries
1 tsp superfine sugar
2 tbsp peanut or sunflower oil
1 tbsp orange juice
½ tsp finely grated orange zest
½ tsp finely grated fresh ginger
salt and black pepper

I Halve the melon and take the seeds out with a spoon. Cut the rind away with a paring knife, then slice the melon thickly. Chill until ready to serve.

2 To make the salsa, hull the strawberries and cut them into large dice. Place in a small mixing bowl with the sugar and crush lightly to release the juices. Add the oil, orange juice, zest, and ginger. Season with salt and a generous twist of black pepper.

3 Arrange the melon on a serving plate, lay the ham over the top, and serve with a bowl of salsa.

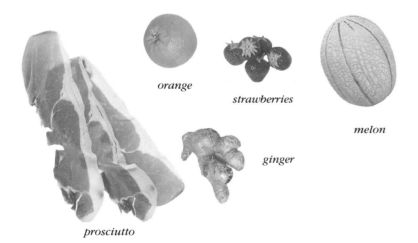

orange

strawberries

melon

ginger

prosciutto

Wild Mushroom Salad with Prosciutto

Fall provides a wealth of new flavors for the salad maker. Most treasured of all are wild mushrooms found mainly in deciduous woodland. If you are not familiar with edible species, larger supermarkets and specialist stores often sell a range of wild and cultivated mushrooms.

Serves 4

INGREDIENTS

6 oz prosciutto, thickly sliced
3 tbsp butter
1 lb wild and cultivated mushrooms
 (chanterelles, shiitake, oyster
 mushrooms, cremini), sliced
4 tbsp brandy
½ oak-leaf lettuce
½ frisée lettuce
1 tbsp walnut oil

HERB PANCAKES

3 tbsp all-purpose flour
5 tbsp milk
1 egg plus 1 egg yolk
4 tbsp freshly grated Parmesan cheese
3 tbsp chopped fresh herbs: parsley,
 thyme, tarragon, marjoram, chives
salt and pepper

frisée lettuce

mushrooms

prosciutto

1 To make the pancakes, combine the flour with the milk in a measuring jug. Beat in the egg and egg yolk with the cheese, herbs, and seasoning. Place a nonstick skillet over a steady heat. Pour in enough mixture to coat the bottom of the pan.

2 When the batter has set, turn the pancake over and cook briefly on the other side. Turn out and cool.

3 Roll the pancakes together and cut into ½ in ribbons. Cut the ham into similar-sized ribbons and toss together with the pancake ribbons.

4 Heat the butter in a skillet until it begins to brown. Add the mushrooms and cook for 6–8 minutes. Add the brandy and ignite with a match. The flames will subside when the alcohol has burned off. Wash and spin the salad leaves, toss with walnut oil, and distribute between 4 plates. Place the ham and pancake ribbons in the center, spoon on the mushrooms, season, and serve warm.

Rockburger Salad with Sesame Croutons

This salad plays on the ingredients that make up the all-American hamburger in a sesame bun. Inside the burger is a special layer of Roquefort, a blue ewe's-milk cheese from France.

COOK'S TIP

If you're planning ahead, it's a good idea to freeze the filled burgers between pieces of waxed paper. They will keep in the freezer for up to 8 weeks.

Serves 4

INGREDIENTS
2 lb lean ground beef
1 egg
1 medium onion, finely chopped
2 tsp French mustard
½ tsp celery salt
black pepper
4 oz Roquefort or other blue cheese
1 large sesame seed bread loaf
3 tbsp olive oil, preferably Spanish
1 small iceberg lettuce
2 oz arugula or watercress
½ cup French Dressing
4 ripe tomatoes, quartered
4 large scallions, sliced

1 Place the ground beef, egg, onion, mustard, celery salt, and pepper in a mixing bowl. Combine thoroughly. Divide the mixture into 16 portions, each weighing about 2 oz.

2 Flatten the pieces between 2 sheets of plastic wrap or waxed paper to form 5 in rounds.

3 Place ½ oz of the cheese on 8 of the thin burgers. Sandwich with the remainder and press the edges firmly. Store between pieces of plastic wrap or waxed paper and chill until ready to cook.

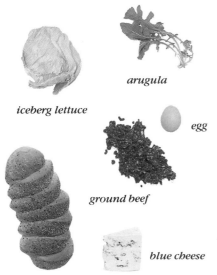

arugula

iceberg lettuce

egg

ground beef

blue cheese

sesame seed bread

4 To make the sesame croutons, pre-heat the broiler to a moderate temperature. Remove the sesame crust from the bread, then cut the crust into short fingers. Brush with olive oil and toast evenly for 10–15 minutes.

5 Season the burgers and broil for 10 minutes, turning once.

6 Wash the salad leaves and spin dry. Toss with the dressing, then distribute between 4 large plates. Place 2 of the rockburgers in the center of each plate and arrange the tomatoes, scallions, and sesame croutons around the edge.

Grilled Chicken Salad with Lavender and Sweet Herbs

Lavender may seem like an odd salad ingredient, but its delightful scent has a natural affinity with sweet garlic, orange, and other wild herbs. A serving of cornmeal polenta makes this salad both filling and delicious.

Serves 4

INGREDIENTS
4 boneless chicken breasts
3¾ cups light chicken stock
1 cup fine polenta or cornmeal
2 oz butter
1 lb young spinach
6 oz lamb's lettuce
8 sprigs fresh lavender
8 small tomatoes, halved
salt and pepper

LAVENDER MARINADE
6 fresh lavender flowers
2 tsp finely grated orange zest
2 cloves garlic, crushed
2 tsp clear honey
salt
2 tbsp olive oil, French or Italian
2 tsp chopped fresh thyme
2 tsp chopped fresh marjoram

lavender *chicken breasts*

1 To make the marinade, strip the lavender flowers from the stems and combine with the orange zest, garlic, honey, and salt. Add the olive oil and herbs. Score the chicken deeply, spread the mixture over the chicken, and leave to marinate in a cool place for at least 20 minutes.

polenta

spinach

orange

garlic

thyme

2 To make the polenta, bring the chicken stock to a boil in a heavy saucepan. Add the cornmeal in a steady stream, stirring all the time until thick: this will take 2–3 minutes. Turn the cooked polenta out on to a 1-in-deep buttered tray and allow to cool.

3 Heat the broiler to a moderate temperature. (If using a barbecue, let the embers settle to a steady glow.) Broil the chicken for 15 minutes, turning once.

4 Cut the polenta into 1 in cubes with a wet knife. Heat the butter in a large skillet and fry the polenta until golden.

COOK'S TIP

Lavender marinade is a delicious flavoring for fish as well as chicken. Try it over broiled cod, haddock, halibut, sea bass, and bream.

5 Wash the salad leaves and spin dry, then divide between 4 large plates. Slice each chicken breast and lay over the salad. Place the polenta among the salad, decorate with sprigs of lavender and tomatoes, season and serve.

Millionaire's Lobster Salad

When money is no object and you're in a decadent mood, this salad will satisfy your every whim. It is ideally served with a cool Chardonnay, Chablis, or Pouilly-Fuissé wine.

Serves 4

INGREDIENTS
1 medium lobster, live or cooked
salt
1 bay leaf
1 sprig thyme
1½ lb new potatoes, scraped
2 ripe tomatoes
4 plump, juicy oranges
½ frisée lettuce
6 oz lamb's lettuce
7 oz can young artichokes in brine, quartered
4 tbsp extra-virgin olive oil
1 small bunch tarragon, chervil, or flat-leaf parsley

DRESSING
2 tbsp frozen concentrated orange juice, thawed
3 oz unsalted butter, diced
salt and cayenne pepper

COOK'S TIP

The rich delicate flavour of this salad depends on using the freshest lobsters. If North Atlantic lobsters (pictured here) are not available, use spiny rock lobsters or crawfish.

new potatoes

lamb's lettuce

lobster

orange

tarragon

tomatoes

frisée lettuce

1 If the lobster needs cooking, bring a large saucepan of salted water to a boil with the bay leaf and thyme. Throw the lobster into the water, return to a boil, and simmer for 15 minutes. Cool under running water. Twist off the legs and claws, and separate the tail piece from the body section. Break the claws open with crackers or a small hammer and remove the meat intact. Cut the tail piece open from the underside with a pair of kitchen shears. Slice the meat and set aside.

2 Bring the potatoes to a boil in salted water and simmer for 20 minutes. Drain, cover, and keep warm. Cover the tomatoes with boiling water and leave for 20 seconds to loosen their skins. Cool under running water and slip off the skins. Halve the tomatoes, discard the seeds, then cut the flesh into large dice.

4 To make the dressing, measure the thawed orange juice into a glass bowl and set it over a saucepan containing 1 in of simmering water. Heat the juice for 1 minute, remove from the heat, then whisk in the butter a little at a time until the dressing reaches a coating consistency. Season to taste with salt and a pinch of cayenne pepper. Cover and keep warm.

3 To segment the oranges, remove the peel from the top, bottom, and sides with a serrated knife. With a small paring knife, loosen the orange segments by cutting between the flesh and the membranes, holding the fruit over a small bowl.

5 Wash the salad leaves and spin dry. Dress with olive oil, then divide between 4 large serving plates. Toss the potatoes, artichokes, and orange segments with olive oil and distribute among the leaves. Lay the sliced lobster over the salad, spoon on the warm butter dressing, add the diced tomato, and decorate with fresh herbs. Serve at room temperature.

Warm Duck Salad with Orange and Cilantro

The rich gamey flavor of duck provides the foundation for this delicious salad. Serve it in late summer or fall and enjoy the warm flavor of orange and cilantro.

Serves 4

INGREDIENTS
1 small orange
2 boneless duck breasts
salt and cayenne pepper
⅔ cup dry white wine
1 tsp ground coriander seeds
½ tsp ground cumin or fennel seeds
2 tbsp superfine sugar
juice of ½ small lime or lemon
3 oz day-old bread, thickly sliced
3 tbsp garlic oil (see Introduction)
½ escarole lettuce
½ frisée lettuce
2 tbsp sunflower or peanut oil
4 sprigs fresh cilantro

1 Halve the orange and slice thickly. Discard any stray seeds and place the slices in a small saucepan. Cover with water, bring to a boil, and simmer for 5 minutes to remove the bitterness. Drain and set aside.

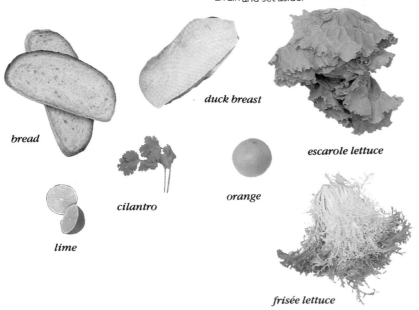

bread

duck breast

escarole lettuce

cilantro

orange

lime

frisée lettuce

2 Pierce the skin of the duck breasts diagonally with a small knife (this will help release the fat as they cook). Rub the skin with salt. Place a steel or cast-iron skillet over a steady heat and cook the breasts for 20 minutes, turning once, until they are medium-rare. Transfer to a warm plate, cover, and keep warm. Pour the duck fat into a small bowl and set aside for use on another occasion.

3 Heat the sediment in the skillet until it begins to darken and caramelize. Add the wine and stir to loosen the sediment. Add the ground coriander, cumin, sugar, and orange slices. Boil quickly and reduce to a coating consistency. Sharpen with lime juice and season to taste with salt and cayenne pepper. Transfer to a bowl, cover, and keep warm.

4 To make the garlic croutons, remove the crusts from the bread and discard them. Cut the bread into short fingers. Heat the garlic oil in a heavy skillet and brown until evenly crisp. Season with salt, then drain on paper towels.

5 Wash the salad leaves and spin dry. Toss with sunflower oil and distribute between 4 large serving plates.

6 Slice the duck breasts diagonally with a carving knife. Divide the breast meat into 4 and lift on to each salad plate. Spoon on the dressing, scatter with croutons, decorate with a sprig of cilantro and serve.

COOK'S TIP

Duck breast has the quality of red meat and is cooked either rare, medium, or well-done according to taste.

Blueberry, Orange, and Lavender Salad

Delicate blueberries emerge here in a simple salad of sharp oranges and little meringues flavored with lavender.

Serves 4

INGREDIENTS
6 oranges
12 oz blueberries
8 sprigs fresh lavender

MERINGUE
2 egg whites
½ cup superfine sugar
1 tsp fresh lavender flowers

egg

blueberries

lavender

orange

1 Preheat the oven to 275°F. Line a baking sheet with 6 layers of newspaper and cover with buttered waxed paper. Whisk the egg whites in a large mixing bowl until they hold their weight on the whisk. Add the sugar a little at a time, whisking thoroughly before each addition. Fold in the lavender flowers.

2 Spoon the meringue into a piping bag fitted with a ¼ in plain nozzle. Pipe as many small buttons of meringue on to the prepared baking sheet as you can. Dry the meringue near the bottom of the oven for 1½–2 hours.

3 To segment the oranges, remove the peel from the top, bottom, and sides with a serrated knife. Loosen the segments by cutting with a paring knife between the flesh and the membranes, holding the fruit over a bowl.

4 Arrange the segments on 4 plates.

5 Combine the blueberries with the lavender meringues and pile in the center of each plate. Decorate with sprigs of lavender and serve.

COOK'S TIP
Lavender is used in both sweet and savory dishes. Always use fresh or recently dried flowers, and avoid artificially scented bunches that are sold for domestic purposes.

Blackberry Salad with Rose Granita

The blackberry is a member of the rose family and combines especially well with rose water. Here a rose syrup is frozen into a granita and served over strips of white meringue.

Serves 4

INGREDIENTS
⅔ cup superfine sugar
1 fresh red rose, petals finely chopped
1 tsp rose water
2 tsp lemon juice
1 lb blackberries
confectioners' sugar, for dusting

MERINGUE
2 egg whites
½ cup superfine sugar

eggs

blackberries

rose

1 Bring ⅔ cup water to a boil in a stainless steel or enamel saucepan. Add the sugar and rose petals, then simmer for 5 minutes. Strain the syrup into a deep metal tray, add a scant 2 cups more water, the rose water and lemon juice, and leave to cool. Freeze the mixture for 3 hours or until solid.

2 Preheat the oven to 275°F. Line a baking sheet with 6 layers of newspaper and cover with buttered waxed paper.

3 For the meringue, whisk the egg whites until they hold their weight on the whisk. Add the superfine sugar a little at a time and whisk until firm.

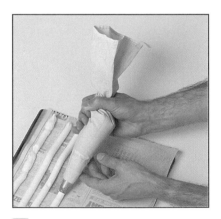

4 Spoon the meringue into a piping bag fitted with a ½ in plain nozzle. Pipe the meringue in lengths across the lined baking sheet. Dry in the bottom of the oven for 1½–2 hours.

5 Break the meringue into 2 in lengths and place 3 or 4 lengths on each of 4 large plates. Pile the blackberries next to the meringue. With a tablespoon, scrape the granita finely. Shape into ovals and place over the meringue. Dust with confectioners' sugar and serve.

Raspberry Salad with Mango Custard Sauce

This remarkable salad unites the sharp quality of fresh raspberries with a special custard made from rich fragrant mangoes.

Serves 4

INGREDIENTS
1 large mango
3 egg yolks
2 tbsp superfine sugar
2 tsp cornstarch
scant 1 cup milk
8 sprigs fresh mint

RASPBERRY SAUCE
1 lb 2 oz raspberries
3 tbsp superfine sugar

eggs

mint

mango

raspberries

1 To prepare the mango, remove the top and bottom with a serrated knife. Cut away the outer skin, then remove the flesh by cutting either side of the flat central pit. Save one half of the fruit for decoration and roughly chop the remainder.

2 For the custard sauce, combine the egg yolks, sugar, cornstarch and 2 tbsp of the milk smoothly in a bowl.

3 Rinse a small saucepan out with cold water to prevent the milk from catching. Bring the rest of the milk to a boil in the pan, pour it over the ingredients in the bowl, and stir evenly.

4 Strain the mixture back into the saucepan, stir to a simmer, and allow the mixture to thicken.

5 Pour the custard sauce into a food processor, add the chopped mango, and blend until smooth. Allow to cool.

COOK'S TIP

Mangoes are ripe when they yield to gentle pressure in the hand. Some varieties show a red-gold or yellow flush when they are ready to eat.

6 To make the raspberry sauce, place 12 oz of the raspberries in a stain-resistant saucepan. Add the sugar, soften over a gentle heat, and simmer for 5 minutes. Force the fruit through a fine nylon strainer to remove the seeds. Allow to cool.

7 Spoon the raspberry sauce and mango custard into 2 pools on 4 plates. Slice the reserved mango and fan out or arrange in a pattern over the raspberry sauce. Scatter fresh raspberries over the mango custard. Decorate with 2 sprigs of mint and serve.

Iced Pineapple Crush with Strawberries and Lychees

The sweet tropical flavors of pineapple and lychees combine well with richly scented strawberries to make this a most refreshing salad.

Serves 4

INGREDIENTS
2 small pineapples
1 lb strawberries
14 oz can lychees
3 tbsp kirsch or white rum
2 tbsp confectioners' sugar

1 Remove the crown from both pineapples by twisting sharply. Reserve the leaves for decoration. p

2 Cut the fruit in half diagonally with a large serrated knife.

pineapple

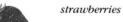

strawberries

3 Cut around the flesh inside the skin with a small serrated knife, keeping the skin intact. Remove the core from the pineapple.

4 Chop the pineapple and combine with the strawberries and lychees, taking care not to damage the fruit.

COOK'S TIP

A ripe pineapple will resist pressure when squeezed and will have a sweet, fragrant smell. In winter freezing conditions can cause the flesh to blacken.

5 Combine the kirsch with the confectioners' sugar, pour over the fruit, and freeze for 45 minutes.

6 Transfer the fruit to the pineapple skins and decorate with pineapple leaves.

Fresh Fig, Apple, and Date Salad

Sweet Mediterranean figs and dates combine especially well with crisp dessert apples. A hint of almond serves to unite the flavors.

Serves 4

INGREDIENTS
6 large apples
juice of ½ lemon
6 oz fresh dates
1 oz white marzipan
1 tsp orange flower water
4 tbsp plain yogurt
4 green or purple figs
4 almonds, toasted

apples

figs   *almonds*

dates

1 Core the apples. Slice thinly, then cut into fine matchsticks. Toss with lemon juice to keep them white.

2 Remove the pits from the dates and cut the flesh into fine strips, then combine with the apple slices.

3 Soften the marzipan with orange flower water and combine with the yogurt. Mix well.

4 Pile the apples and dates in the center of 4 plates. Remove the stem from each of the figs and divide the fruit into quarters without cutting right through the base. Squeeze the base with the thumb and forefinger of each hand to open up the fruit.

5 Place a fig in the center of the salad, spoon in the yogurt filling, and decorate with a toasted almond.

Muscat Grape Frappé

The flavor and perfume of the Muscat grape is rarely more enticing than when captured in this icy-cool salad. Because of its alcohol content, this dish is not suitable for young children.

Serves 4

INGREDIENTS
½ bottle Muscat wine, Beaumes de
    Venise, Frontignan, or Rivsaltes
1 lb Muscat grapes

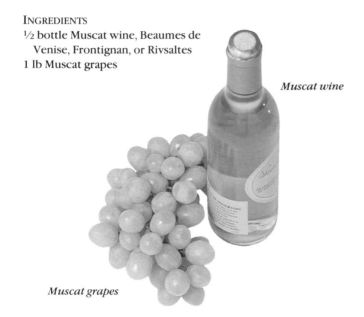

Muscat wine

Muscat grapes

1 Pour the wine into a stainless-steel or enamel tray, add ⅔ cup water and freeze for 3 hours or until completely solid.

2 Remove the seeds from the grapes with a pair of tweezers. If you have time, peel the grapes.

3 Scrape the frozen wine with a spoon to make a fine ice. Combine the grapes with the ice and spoon into 4 shallow glasses.

Grapefruit Salad with Campari and Orange

The bittersweet flavor of Campari combines especially well with citrus fruit. Because of its alcohol content, this dish is not suitable for young children.

Serves 4

INGREDIENTS
3 tbsp superfine sugar
4 tbsp Campari
2 tbsp lemon juice
4 grapefruit
5 oranges
4 sprigs fresh mint

COOK'S TIP

When buying citrus fruit, choose brightly colored varieties that feel heavy for their size.

grapefruit

mint

oranges

lemon juice

Campari

1 Bring ⅔ cup water to a boil in a small saucepan, add the sugar, and simmer until dissolved. Cool in a metal tray, then add the Campari and lemon juice. Chill until ready to serve.

2 Cut the peel from the top, bottom, and sides of the grapefruit and oranges with a serrated knife. Segment the fruit into a bowl by slipping a small paring knife between the flesh and the membranes. Combine the fruit with the Campari syrup and chill.

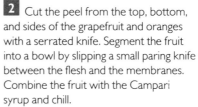

3 Spoon the salad into 4 dishes and finish with a sprig of fresh mint.

Strawberries with Raspberry and Passion Fruit Sauce

Fragrant strawberries release their finest flavor when moistened with a sauce of fresh raspberries and scented passion fruit.

Serves 4

INGREDIENTS
12 oz raspberries, fresh or frozen
3 tbsp superfine sugar
1 passion fruit
1½ lb small strawberries
8 plain butter cookies, to serve

cookies

passion fruit

raspberries

strawberries

I Place the raspberries and sugar in a stain-resistant saucepan and soften over a gentle heat to release the juices. Simmer for 5 minutes. Allow to cool.

2 Halve the passion fruit and scoop out the seeds and juice.

3 Transfer the raspberries into a food processor or blender, add the passion fruit, and blend smoothly.

COOK'S TIP
Berry fruits offer their best flavor when served at room temperature.

4 Force the fruit sauce through a fine nylon strainer to remove the seeds.

5 Fold the strawberries into the sauce, then spoon into 4 stemmed glasses. Serve with plain butter cookies.

Mixed Melon Salad with Wild Strawberries

Ice-cold melon is a delicious way to end a meal. Here several varieties are combined with strongly flavored wild strawberries. If wild berries are not available, use ordinary strawberries or raspberries.

Serves 4

INGREDIENTS
1 cantaloupe or charentais melon
1 galia or Spanish melon
2 lb watermelon
6 oz wild strawberries
4 sprigs fresh mint

wild strawberries

galia melon

mint

cantaloupe

watermelon

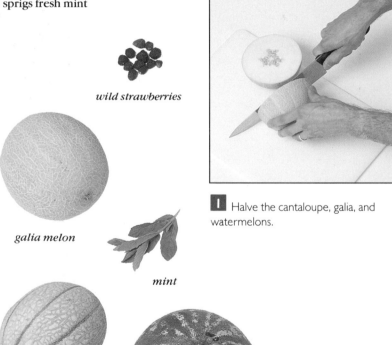

COOK'S TIP
Ripe melons should give slightly when pressed at the base, and should give off a fruity, melony scent. Buy carefully if you plan to use the fruit on the day.

1 Halve the cantaloupe, galia, and watermelons.

2 Remove the seeds from the cantaloupe and galia with a spoon.

3 With a melon-baller, take out as many balls as you can from all 3 melons. Combine in a large bowl and refrigerate.

4 Add the wild strawberries and transfer to 4 stemmed glass dishes.

5 Decorate with sprigs of mint.

INDEX